HABITS of Resistance

ELIZABETH
WOODSON

7 Ways You're Being Formed by Culture & Gospel Practices to Help You Push Back

HABITS of Resistance

PUBLISHING®
BRENTWOOD, TENNESSEE

Copyright © 2026 by Elizabeth Woodson
All rights reserved.
Printed in the United States of America

979-8-3845-0852-6

Published by B&H Publishing Group
Brentwood, Tennessee

Dewey Decimal Classification: 234.4
Subject Heading: CHRISTIAN LIFE / REGENERATION (CHRISTIANITY) / DISCIPLESHIP

Unless otherwise noted, all Scripture is taken from the Christian Standard Bible, copyright © 2017 by Holman Bible Publishers. Used by permission. Christian Standard Bible®, and CSB® are federally registered trademarks of Holman Bible Publishers, all rights reserved.

Scripture references marked CEV are taken from the Contemporary English Version, copyright © 1995 by American Bible Society For more information about CEV, visit www.bibles.com and www.cev.bible.

Scripture marked NIV are taken from the New International Version®, NIV® Copyright ©1973, 1978, 1984, 2011 by Biblica, Inc.® Used by permission. All rights reserved worldwide.

Cover design and illustration by B&H Publishing Group.
Author photo by Kauwuane Burton.

1 2 3 4 5 6 • 29 28 27 26

To those whose hearts ache for more in life and in their walk with God but are unsure of where to find it.

Acknowledgments

This book is the fruit of years of study, teaching, reading, and thoughtful conversations. The opportunity to do all of this was, in part, made possible during my time working at The Village Church Institute. Thank you J. T. for believing in me and giving me the space to soar.

I also want to acknowledge the friends and family who have wrestled with me in conversation, challenged my ideas, and joined me to revel in the beauty of shalom and the God who created it.

Contents

Introduction

The Wrong Door

When I was younger, I was an avid reader. One series I enjoyed reading was the Choose Your Own Adventure books, an interactive series that allows the reader to choose the outcome of the story. Each story provided some type of adventure, taking the reader to exciting destinations like the Amazon, Stonehenge, or outer space to solve a mystery. What made this book series unique was that at the end of every chapter, the reader was given two page numbers, each leading to different sections of the story. One page number might take you to a section where you uncover an important clue. Another might take you to a section where you die tragically. For this reason, I had the bad habit of turning to both pages and choosing the best outcome! *(Don't judge me, you would have done the same.)* Even though I sometimes looked ahead, I remember loving these books because they provided me with an opportunity to go on an adventure toward the pages that would give me the best experience and choose the pathway to get there.

As believers, our lives resemble these Choose Your Own Adventure books. Each morning, we wake up looking for a new "adventure." Our actions are motivated by the goal of reaching a specific destination. The way we allocate our time, spend our money, and the activities we opt into and out of are all pointed toward one goal—the good life.

For some of us, this looks like a simple desire to live life to the fullest, experiencing all the joy that is available to us. For others, it is a desire for significance and belonging. We want to know that our life matters, while experiencing a life where we are known and loved. For others, it could be a desire for the pain in our life to stop. Whether it's from a broken relationship, difficult job situation, or physical ailment, we want to be relieved of the pain we are experiencing. Still others of us find ourselves asking a very simple question: Is this all that there is? Life feels endlessly mundane and ordinary, with a mind-numbing consistency that has become overwhelming and suffocating.

In some sense, all these struggles point to good core desires we have as humans. All of us want love, hope, joy, peace, and a myriad of other virtuous things. However, if we were to peel back the layers and examine what we think our life is lacking, we would find that what we seek is actually a desire for wholeness or a deep state of well-being where our life has meaning and purpose. We recognize something about life is not as it should be, and even though we don't have the words to fully describe it, we just want what feels "off" to be made right.

I believe our desire for the good life is really a desire for the biblical concept of ***shalom***.

I will spend time unpacking the word *shalom* later in this book, but for now I will offer this short definition: *Shalom is a life of wholeness and delight, where everything is as it ought to be.*

Every day we are given two different options for how to achieve the good life or shalom. Picture two doors that lead to two different paths that will end at two different destinations. Each door presents a promise of salvation, a proclamation of good news that we can be rescued from our situation and delivered to our desired destination. One door presents a false gospel that will lead us down the way of the world (James 3:15). The other door presents the true gospel, that will lead us down the way of Christ (James 3:17–18).

Our problem is that we are choosing the wrong door.

Rotten Fruit

Have you ever opened your refrigerator to be met with a scent so bad that it hits you right in your face? As soon as you open the door, you immediately realize that something inside has passed its expiration date and needs to be found and discarded quickly! If you are anything like me, when this happens, you drop everything to do a mad dash search through the fridge to discover and dispose of the bad-scent culprit. However, if I wait too long to deal with it, the scent starts to seep out of the fridge into my kitchen; it's the worst!

As believers, our lives produce a spiritual scent or aroma that helps us gauge the quality or health of our relationship with God (2 Cor. 2:15). The closer we are to Christlikeness, the sweeter the aroma. But as we start to move in the other direction, that sweet smell can quickly turn sour. In Galatians 5:22–23, the apostle Paul writes that the fruit of the Spirit is, "love, joy, peace, patience, kindness, goodness, faithfulness, gentleness, and self-control." So anytime we see our life producing characteristics opposite of these, we are getting that first whiff of "rotting fruit" that is coming out of our spiritual refrigerator.

Now, you might be thinking, *Elizabeth, what does this have to do with the two doors?* Well, I believe that the scent some of our lives are giving off is a little sour. It is signaling that our spiritual health might not be as fresh as it should be. The reason for this is that we are not choosing the door that leads us to the way of Christ but the one that is leading us to the way of the world. There are numerous examples of this, but this one is worth noting: the conversations we participate in. These can easily serve as indicators for our spiritual health—especially if we pay attention to how we show up online. When I consider some of what I've heard and seen online, I think the spiritual aroma many of us are giving off is that of anger, discontentment, and fear.

Anger

I am writing this book as America prepares for another presidential election. Politics is often seen as a topic to be avoided in conversation at all costs. Over the past few presidential election cycles, political conversations have gone from frustrating to infuriating. Regardless of what political party a person supports, disagreement with members of the opposing party is usually met with vitriolic anger, and sometimes even violence (e.g., January 6, 2021 insurrection). Whether online or in person, our discussions about politics from the past few years have eroded our ecclesial unity and caused seemingly irreparable chasms in our close relationships. Behind these rifts is a deep sense of anger that hasn't been dealt with in our hearts. This divisiveness has also found its way into other disagreements about doctrine, public and private school, racism, justice, and other conversations related to Christian living. It seems like it is getting harder and harder for Christians to honor those they disagree with, or to put it in the Bible's terms, "to slander no one, to avoid fighting, and to be kind, always showing gentleness to all people" (Titus 3:2).

Discontentment

The internet also constantly entices us with images and videos that display the life we should aspire to have. Whether it's the latest tech gadget, a kitchen remodel, or the family that has perfect photos with matching outfits, our constant engagement with other people's lives is a breeding ground for comparison that then leads to discontentment. As we are comparing our lives to the things we see online, we are made to believe that what they have is better and that what we have is not enough. We spend more to buy the things we see to help achieve the life we want. But the effects of our materialism are short-lived, and we end up back at the door of discontentment the next time we see something we want but don't have.[1]

Fear

In 2023, the Surgeon General declared loneliness as a national epidemic.[2] Even though the internet connects us digitally, so many of us remain disconnected relationally. Studies show that over the past few years, there has been an increase in the amount of people who are experiencing mental health struggles, specifically depression and anxiety. Our discontentment has served as a catalyst for this growth, but so has stress from major life events from the past few years like the COVID pandemic and ongoing economic instability. For some, it seems as if life has passed them by and their inability to catch up or overcome has left them overwhelmed with uncertainty about the future.[3]

This is likely not news to you. The topic of how social media and our use of technology is changing us is well-documented. Many books have been written that show a correlation between our social media usage and our lived experience.[4] They detail how we are being formed in the image that our phones reflect to us, which shows up in our increased love or acceptance of: immediate gratification, complacency with our sin, FOMO, and harsh communication.

But what is interesting is that our social media usage is outpacing our time in discipleship environments. The average person spends about 2.5 hours a day or 17.5 hours a week on social media. Now, think about how much time the average Christian spends in discipleship environments, including church services, small groups, Bible studies, and daily quiet times. Even if it is an hour a day, which is likely above average, that person is spending more than twice this amount of time on social media.[5]

Furthermore, since the end of the pandemic in 2021, there has been a sizable decrease in the number of adults who are engaging the Scriptures, whether daily, weekly, or just a few times a year.[6] We are spending less time in the book that helps form the foundation of our faith. Additionally, even when we read Scripture, we're not always equipped to understand and apply biblical teaching.[7] Research shows that many Christians hold unbiblical views on key doctrinal issues like Jesus, humanity, sin, and salvation.[8]

We are spending more time and mental energy in our social media formational environments than the environments that form us in our Christian faith. Even if we are attending church weekly, participating in a small group and doing a daily quiet time—all of this is not necessarily correlating to a deep abiding knowledge of God's Word if our time with God is overshadowed by our time spent online.

Simply put, we are continually choosing the wrong door because we are growing to be more familiar and more enticed by the stories of our culture than the story of the Bible. The stories we believe matter, our habits reveal that we are consuming the wrong ones, and it is shaping us deeply.

We Love Stories

For the longest time, I always wondered why people loved Hallmark movies. After all, they all seem to have the same predictable plot. With each movie, the same thing happens—boy meets girl, they fall in love, break up, and then, after overcoming a seemingly insurmountable obstacle, they get back together forever. I couldn't understand the allure until a few years ago when I watched a handful of Hallmark movies back-to-back with my sister.

As we watched the second or third movie, it suddenly clicked for me. Over and over again, I saw what people love—the thrill of a budding relationship, the exhilaration of overcoming obstacles, and the deep satisfaction of two people ending up "happily ever after." With each new movie, these scenes evoked an emotional response from me that never got old. At that moment, I realized these movies were so popular because they painted a picture of what we all long to have—"the good life," or the place where we think true happiness is found.[9]

For generations, humanity has communicated the truth about their existence from the perspective of a character in a narrative whose story continues to unfold. As humans, we have a built-in narrative instinct, as if we have been designed to use stories to remember our past, make sense of our present, and shape our future.[10] We interpret our life experiences through stories, a collection of facts seen through the lens of our mind, body, and heart. Stories help us make sense of the world and find our place within it, answering the three core life questions all of us ask: *Who am I? Why am I here? Where do I belong?*

However, we aren't born with these stories. Over the years, they are shaped by various influences. The TV shows we watch, the people we follow on social media, and our community all teach us how to view our lives and the world we live in. They tell us what to value, how to view the people around us, and how we should steward the resources we have been given.

Moreover, every story has its own version of heaven, hell, and a Savior figure. We can see this in the Hallmark movies I struggle to watch. In these stories, heaven is romantic bliss, hell is remaining alone, and the Savior figure who gets you over the bridge from hell to heaven is a prince in a made-up country who happens to meet you at your small-town apple stand. By telling us how the Savior figure will help us escape hell and make it to heaven, every story ultimately shows us where "the good life" can be found.

You and I are like sponges, absorbing the information we expose ourselves to the most. So if our minds and hearts are primarily fixated on our surrounding culture, we will use its various stories to answer the questions we have about our human longings. We will look to them to figure out where to find love, our identity, and even hope in the midst of suffering. While we should continue to ask, *Who am I? Why am I here? Where do I belong?*, our habits are leading us to look for answers in the wrong place.

Remember when I said that our questions about flourishing are really a search for shalom? When we use the map provided by our culture, we are setting out toward a destination we will never reach. What culture doesn't tell you is that their solution is really a trojan horse, a door that does not lead to shalom, but that instead leads us to reject the One through whom shalom is found.

The False Gospel of Our Age | Radical Expressive Individualism

I am rarely running early; usually I am running late. But last year, I left my house a little earlier than usual. I was on my way to church to teach in our women's Bible study. As I walked down my steps to the place my car was parked, I did what I always do—hit the little button on my key remote to open my car door. When I press the button, my car makes a beep sound that lets me know the doors are unlocked. However, this time, when I hit the button, I didn't hear the beep sound. I immediately stopped in my tracks because this meant one thing—my car battery was dead.

After confirming that my suspicions were in fact true, I opened my phone to order an Uber. I needed to get to church, and my car battery issues would have to wait until I was done. In about five minutes my ride pulled up and I quickly got inside. My driver's name was Rickey, and let's just say he was real chatty!

We started making small talk, commenting on the weather and how his day was going. He had a strikingly positive disposition, so I pressed in to learn why. Rickey began to share about how he believed we can control what happens in our lives. Through the power of positive thinking, we can overcome what is going on in the world. He wasn't a Christian, but rather a "spiritual person" who was trying to live his best life. As Rickey talked and I listened, it became apparent that he believed his good feelings were the guide that he needed to get to his desired destination. As long as he listened to the voice inside of him, he would be okay.

Maybe you've talked to someone who sounds a little bit like Rickey—they are "spiritual but not religious," driven by a guide that is hidden inside of them. They believe the pursuit of authenticity will lead them to the good life they are looking for.

This mindset is the calling card of our culture's narrative, which we could call the (false) Gospel of Radical Individualism. It is the belief that the pathway to the flourishing we seek comes through us centering ourselves and it has three key elements:[11]

1. **We "Decenter" God So We Can Be God:** As we move away from the things of God, we slowly begin to prioritize the voices of others over the voice of God. These voices tell us that the pathway to our best life is inside of us—that we must turn inward to cultivate and discover our true self.[12]

2. **Do What Feels Good:** When we decenter God and center ourselves, we begin to be motivated or driven by what feels good to us, pleases us, and doesn't make us uncomfortable. Since we are our greatest authority, we are hesitant to allow external influences that might seek to limit us and hold us back.

3. **Live Like This World Is All There Is:** With our time and our money, we pursue what feels good to us here and now because that's all there is. Our driving motivations lead us to find our identity in things like success, our careers, comfort, and the acquisition of material things.

Every story has an ending, and while this one makes us believe we can find our best life simply by staying true to ourselves, it sadly leads us to a place that is more sinister than we could imagine. This is because it's a place where we are serving the storylines of this world rather than the God who created us.

Don't Get Hustled

When I think about our culture's narrative of radical individualism, there is always one detail that is left out of the story—the cost. Through all the information that is pushed our way, we are given a seemingly beautiful vision about the potential of autonomy. The opportunity to be free to choose our own way as the captain of our own lives is an enticing offer. People seem so empowered, embracing who they are as they courageously chart their own course.

But, with all the effort that is used to spread this false gospel, there is an even greater effort exerted to ensure we never consider what it will cost us and others. We are never encouraged to wrestle with the truth that by following this way we will eventually reject God and mistreat others.[13] Instead of finding shalom, we will live a life without it.

Sadly, because of where you (and I) are located and the time period you live in, this story is your (and my) default setting. It is where you will naturally lean in the pursuit of your human longings of identity, love, peace, hope, and more. It's the story you think will get you the good life, as long as you walk according to its script. Here's a secret though: You don't learn this story all at once, as if you were watching a movie. You receive it slowly in pieces, downloaded to your heart and mind with each click, swipe, and download. You are shaped by it over time and through a cumulative and compounding experience, over years and years. To combat this false story—and many others—it's high time you (and I) start not only engaging with our culture's content actively, but comparing it to a better story and a better way. The Jesus story, and the Jesus way.

Moreover, unless you are intentional about not only *knowing* the false stories swirling around you, but *resisting* them so that you might be formed by a better one, you *will* be formed according to the way of the world. There is no middle ground or gray area. Either passively choose lesser ways and lesser stories that will fail you and malform you, or actively resist those false options and persistently form your life according to the way and story of Jesus.

This is why I wrote this book: to help you learn how to resist. The Gospel of Jesus Christ is the best option for our flourishing. In the midst of the false stories we are faced with every day, we must learn how to interrogate and deconstruct the stories of our culture through the lens of the gospel. As we do this, we won't just identify our culture's false stories and ways—we'll also start building habits of resistance that weaken the grip those stories have on our lives.

Our journey will be twofold:

First, we will *learn to deconstruct the stories of our culture.* We will do this by first taking a contemplative look at the Genesis creation narrative. By examining this story with fresh eyes, we'll learn how everything we desire was created by God for us to enjoy with him. We will then learn to examine our culture's stories in light of the gospel by asking critical questions. We will see how these stories form us, what they tell us is true about God, and where they tell us the good life can be found. Through our questions we'll come to learn why what our culture promises us pales in comparison to what the gospel provides.

Second, we will *learn to live in the story of the Bible.* Our plan of resistance isn't just about information accumulation but about transformation. Alongside training our minds and hearts to believe that our culture's stories are untrue and inferior, we must train our minds and hearts to believe that God's story is better. We will do this by spending time in a few key moments in the life of Israel, seeing the fruit of God's constant presence in their lives. We'll see that it is by remaining in relationship with him, we can access the overflow of shalom we long for.

How?, you may wonder. Once we identify the false stories of our culture and remember to walk in Christ's story and Christ's way, how do we *stay* in his story? What's the secret to resisting the false gospels and walking according to the true one? Habits. Remember, we are slowly formed into our culture's false narratives through our habits—which means we can slowly de-form ourselves *out* of them, breaking free from their hold over our imagination, so that we might reenter the story of God and enjoy relationship with him.

Since Jesus shows us how to be in relationship with God, expect to learn from him in the coming pages, seeing how following his way helps learn how these habits transform us and lead us to shalom. And at the end of each chapter, I will help you apply those teachings by sharing one of the spiritual habits the church has practiced for centuries. After all, this plan of resistance wasn't created by me; rather, it's something the church has historically practiced since its inception.

A Few Final Words . . .

1. **This is a book for you to read in community:** Your first response after reading it shouldn't be to tell other people how they need to get it together. It's designed for you to consider how you are being shaped and formed. But that process of consideration or contemplation is best done in a group of people because we learn more when we do it in community. So read this book with some friends. Talk about the cultural narratives I present, wrestle with the observations I pull

out of the biblical text, and commit to live out the spiritual disciplines I share with you together.

2. **My audience is my spiritual little brothers and sisters:** While I think everyone can benefit from this book, I do have an audience in mind. I am writing to my little brothers and sisters, Christians who are millennial, Gen Z, or younger. You engage faith and religion differently than previous generations. You ask thoughtful questions that are making the church a better place. But, with all love, you are also getting bamboozled by seemingly good things. I want you to experience the biblical vision of shalom and am worried about the ways the world is pulling you away from it (or selling you a false version of it that will only leave you exhausted and miserable).

To end this chapter, let's consider the powerful words of Josh Chatraw:

> Contrasting the Christian story with these rival narratives sobers us to the way we are actually living despite what we confess. To counter these stories, we must embed our lives in the true story. Through the reading of the Scriptures, the fellowship of the saints, the partaking of the sacraments, daily prayers,

> and the preaching of the Word, God reorients the way we see the world. Constantly comparing the rival stories to God's story is essential to not being lulled to sleep in a secular age.[14]

Friend, too many of us are being lulled to sleep. It's time to wake up!

Are you ready to walk through the right and true door? To land on the only path that delivers on its promise to give you the good life? To learn the habits that can break you free from the lies of the false stories whispered in your ear all day long, ushering you into the truest story and greatest adventure you've ever known? To arrive at true shalom instead of being constantly disappointed by counterfeits?

I know I am! Let's go!

Chapter 1

A Better Peace

During my freshman year of college, I got a phone call from my mom with unexpected news. She told me that my high school friend Gena[1] had just stopped by the house to talk with her and my dad. Gena told them about how she and her family were moving to another state. She was devastated by the news, since she was about to start her senior year of high school. In her attempt to remedy the situation, Gena talked to her parents about the possibility of finding another family to live with temporarily so she wouldn't have to switch schools. After spending several minutes laying out her story, she then proceeded to ask my parents if she could stay with them. Without hesitation, my parents graciously told her no.

While Gena's request sounds a little wild, my friend was doing her best to remedy a bad situation. However, her plan had one blind spot—the lack of information she had about my family. What she didn't know is that we had moved around a lot, so my parents knew kids could be resilient when changing schools. This meant that when they heard Gena's sad story, they weren't likely to be overly sympathetic. Even though she had tried her hardest to regain control of her situation, it slipped right out of her hands.

At one time or another, like my friend Gena, we have all had our lives disrupted by something unexpected. It could be a challenging health diagnosis, the loss of a job, or family tension that lasts longer that we would have hoped. I don't know about you, but when a disruption comes my way, I quickly jump into research mode. I find myself hoping my deep dives on Google will help me troubleshoot and create a plan to solve my new problem. The planning process is empowering! It helps ease some of our anxiousness as we attempt to get our situation back under control.

I used to think that the thing the whole world was chasing was control. But when I thought more about it, I realized that control is one step short of the thing we actually want when life has been interrupted. What we really want is for our control tactics to give us *peace.*

Peace is often described as a state of existence that is free from anxiety or disruption. We tend to experience it only when the noise, chaos, or frustration from our situation starts to subside. It might be a quiet moment in the morning before the rest of your family gets up or a silent ride on a plane made possible by your noise-canceling headphones. As we sit in our comfy chair enjoying a hot cup of coffee or look out the window to see the sun setting over the clouds, we pause to reflect on the calm that has been brought our way.

Unfortunately, however, these moments of peace don't usually last long. Soon, we get interrupted by life and are thrust back into the hustle and bustle that remind us of the peace we once had and long to regain.

In fact, sometimes the absence of peace tends to linger with us longer than peace itself does. We all know what it feels like. It's a subtle but persistent sense of dread or self-doubt that is accompanied by worrying thoughts that cycle through our minds on repeat. Other times, it's feelings of anxiousness or tension that start in our gut and appear through raised shoulders, a clenched jaw, and headaches. It makes us distracted, eats away at our sleep, and if it stays too long, our minds and bodies will shift into survival mode as we try to protect ourselves against any danger we perceive, both present and future.

A lack of peace produces a myriad of uncomfortable feelings. We hate to be uncomfortable, so it's understandable that we would want to do anything in our power to relieve this tension. We just want to return to what life was like before the chaos arrived.

Back to the Beginning

Like I mentioned in the previous chapter, we will begin our deconstruction of our culture's false stories by taking a fresh look at Genesis 1–4. Since Scripture creates the foundation for what we believe about the world, these first four chapters help give us renewed vision for what God created us to experience. My hope is that each time we look at the story, you will see how our core desires were designed to be fulfilled in the environment of shalom God created for us. I also hope you see how drastically things changed when sin entered the equation.

We'll start by taking a fresh look at the shift that happens in Genesis 3, which is a little jarring. In only a few verses, a moment of pure bliss in Genesis 2:23–25 transitions to a moment of difficulty and hardship in Genesis 3:16–24. The story moves from Adam and Eve thriving in Eden to them being evicted from that same garden bearing a new reality that is marked by the curses God gives to them.

As the Creator of the universe, God's curses are not unfair but rather are the natural consequences of Adam and Eve's choice to be the determiners of their own fate instead of loyal followers of God. In five verses, God provides the harrowing details of what their new life will be like. With words and phrases like, "labor pains," "painful effort," "thorns and thistles," and "sweat of your brow," it becomes quickly apparent that Adam and Eve's new lives will be characterized by one thing: struggle. Even though Genesis describes their pre-fall reality, we don't know how good Adam and Eve had it until we see in these verses how bad things would be.

Before the fall, with ease our children would be birthed, relationships would be sustained, the ground would be cultivated and cooperate with us—not to mention that instead of experiencing death, we would live forever. Life was supposed to be easy, calm, tranquil, and perfect. Adam and Eve were created to live in paradise. We see glimpses of this in the description of Eden, as Moses tells us that the rivers that went out from the garden were near lands that had precious stones like gold, bdellium, and onyx (Gen. 2:10–14).

There is no place more peaceful than paradise. But our experience of it was only possible under the rule of God. Adam and Eve's disobedience left them banished from Eden with the challenge of trying to figure out life outside of paradise. Instead of having an unbroken experience of tranquility, their lives will continually be interrupted by difficulty—the fruit of a world impacted by sin. Consequently, they will also continue to fight against the self-empowerment temptation the serpent offered them. As their sons and daughters, we fight against the same temptation, striving to regain peace by figuring out life on our own, apart from God.

Our Culture's Story: *Peace Through Control*

Each year, the most used dictionaries like *Merriam-Webster*, Dictionary.com, and the *Oxford Dictionary* choose a word of the year. According to Dictionary.com, the word of the year is determined by their lexicographers, the people who compile dictionaries. They analyze a large amount of data to identify words that make an impact on our conversations. The words that make it to the top of the list usually highlight the social trends and global events that defined the year.[2]

While some of the words from the past few years, like *demure*, relate to a fun viral video, others tell a more interesting story about our habits and the way we try to bring our lives back into a state of peace by controlling them.

Manifest

In 2024, the word *manifest* was searched 130,000 times in the *Cambridge Dictionary*, making it their word of the year. *Manifest* is defined as the use of "methods such as visualization . . . and affirmation . . . to help you imagine achieving something you want, in the belief that doing so will make it more likely to happen . . ."[3]

As a word in our English vernacular, *manifest* has been around since the early 1300s. However, it was not until the 2020 pandemic that the word's usage skyrocketed in our global culture. Popularized by celebrities like Simone Biles, Oprah, and Ariana Grande, posts and videos about manifesting spread quickly on social media. Whether it was a new relationship, job, movie role, or Olympic medal, people began explaining their success, using the phrase "I manifested this." This then gave rise to different manifestation experts and influencers who, for a small nominal price, could help you learn how to make your dreams reality.

Connected to other self-help movements like the power of positive thinking and the law of attraction, manifestation invites you to believe that you can turn your dreams into reality through the following steps:[4]

1. Visualize your desires, being specific about whatever it is that you want.
2. Ask the universe or a higher power for it, which can happen through prayer, meditation, or a vision board.

3. Start working toward your goals in "co-creating" with the universe or your higher power.
4. Attract your desires by cultivating positivity, using affirmations, or practicing gratitude.

Here's the thing: Outside of "co-creating" with the universe, these steps are not entirely untrue or unable to bring any positive change to your life. Creating a plan, praying about that plan, and taking intentional steps to accomplish the plan all while remaining positive will sometimes produce the results you want. The problem is that these steps create a formula of sorts that seems to provide a *no-fail* plan to achieve our best lives. So much so, that when people say "I manifested this" it sounds like by the magic of their hard work and good planning they made whatever they wanted to appear. It is as if they are Vanna White from *Wheel of Fortune* making a letter on the screen appear with the simple touch of a finger.

But formulas are only as good as their inputs, and manifesting assumes you control all the inputs.

Formed by Culture

When our lives are devoid of peace, our culture's false story of self-empowerment leads us to believe that we can resolve our situation through our own diligence and tenacity. Yet this pathway has hidden costs and disadvantages that are rarely shared when presented.

For example, some people who claim to have manifested a profitable business after quitting their 9-to-5 job leave out a few important details. They don't mention the money they saved up before they quit or the large network they built while still working their 9-to-5 that was used to promote their product. Their well-curated Instagram video and coaching course gives you the impression that all it took was visualization, positivity, and hard work. In reality, a good portion of their success may have come from life circumstances that gave them a unique advantage.

On the other hand, while being intentional about our life choices can get us closer to our goals, sometimes, no matter how hard we work, things do not go in our favor. We can do all the things to manifest good health and still get cancer. We can try to manifest a spouse and stay single for years. Sadly, when the formula we've created doesn't work, we rarely question the formula but attribute our failure to user error. This makes us insecure and fragile, as we turn inward when life goes in an unexpected direction. Instead of blaming the formula for misleading us, we blame ourselves. After ruminating on our inadequacies, we are left wondering, *If I can't work my way out of a difficult situation, then what hope do I have that things will get better?*

If this weren't enough, self-empowerment's invitation to solve our problems through unlimited information doesn't include the disclaimer that the people we will learn from might not be telling the truth. While we may have access to all the answers we could ever want, we will still be responsible for deciphering which ones are the best or the most truthful. As we embrace the path of self-education, we will learn a great deal of information, but lack the wisdom required to use our knowledge well. Both online and offline, our overconfidence will cause us to misapply our knowledge in ways that are disastrous.

The false gospel of self-empowerment promises that we can control our lives and thereby attain our own peace, a belief that assumes that on our own we can see well enough to navigate through the world. But the inescapable reality is that our control and our vision is limited because *we* are limited. No matter how good our plan is, we can never account for the unexpected things life will throw our way.

What if instead of trusting in our limited abilities to obtain our peace, we trust in the One who is limitless?

God's Story: *Peace Through Surrender*

One of the beautiful things about the Old Testament is that it helps us see God's character on display. Specifically, through his interactions with the nation of Israel, we see how God's continual presence in their life fulfills the core desires they need and long for. That is to say, with God's "here-forever presence comes his here-forever wisdom, his here-forever grace, his here-forever strength, his here-forever authority, his here-forever love, his here-forever mercy, his here-forever righteousness, and his here-forever patience. . . . [God's] presence guarantees that in [our] suffering, [we] will have everything [we] need."[5]

Similar to what we did with the "Back to the Beginning" section, in each chapter we will look at moments in the life of humanity post-Eden. As Israel is learning, and at times struggling, to be the people of God, we will see how God's consistent character is a reminder that all they need they have in him.

Let's start with one of the events in the Old Testament that gets repeated *frequently*.

Whenever the history of the people of Israel is being told, the story of God delivering Israel out of slavery always makes the list. Its frequent use means that this event is one of Israel's core memories, something that has indelibly shaped how they view the world and their place in it.

This story, which takes place at the beginning of Exodus, describes how Israel is enslaved in Egypt. God sends a man named Moses to help deliver them. God's plan of deliverance involves Moses and his brother Aaron, as they repeatedly visit Pharaoh and ask for Israel's freedom. Their request was always accompanied with the caveat that if Pharaoh said "no," God would send plagues or natural disasters to cause Egypt to suffer.

Ten times Pharaoh is asked to release Israel and ten times he refuses. God responds by sending ten different plagues to afflict the Egyptian people. These plagues include the water in the Nile River turning to blood, a frog infestation, the dust of the earth turning into gnats, flies filling their homes, all the livestock dying, Egyptians being afflicted with painful boils and sores, large hail raining down, locusts that destroyed all the plants and trees, three days of complete darkness, and finally the death of the firstborn of each Egyptian family.

However, these ten plagues were not random. Each plague corresponded to one of the gods of Egypt who governed that part of nature. For example, Hapi was the Egyptian god of the Nile.[6] So when the Nile was turned to blood, it would have been seen as a direct attack against him. With each plague, God was repeatedly showing how he was greater than anyone and anything, including the false gods of Egypt.

This mighty expression of God's sovereignty and omnipotence was brought to a climax in Exodus 14. After having set Israel free, Pharaoh changes his mind and decides to chase after them. Israel finds themselves trapped between Pharaoh's armies and the Red Sea. But, by the power of God, Moses splits the Red Sea open so Israel can walk to the other side on dry ground. As Pharaoh and his army followed Israel into the water, it closed in on them and they drowned. At the end of this epic battle between Pharaoh and God, God was the only one left standing. What was impossible for Israel to accomplish on their own proved to be possible for God.

Every time Israel repeated this story, it ingrained in their minds that God's power and authority was unmatched; he alone was in control. And, while they were limited, they served a God who was limitless, which meant nothing would be impossible for him! By God's own strong arm and sovereign control over the circumstances, Israel was led out of danger and into a place God designed for them to have peace (Lev. 26:3–6).

Formed by God

There are a few moments in my life that stand out as core memories that were extremely impactful to me. One of them took place during my senior year of college. I was a business major with high hopes of becoming a CPA who used my skills for the kingdom of God. Somehow, I came across the name of an alum (Jeff) from my college who worked for a non-profit organization. I was curious about his experience, so I sent him an email asking to meet up. Honestly, I didn't have huge hopes for this meeting. I saw it more as a networking opportunity, believing that he could introduce me to someone who would then introduce me to someone else who might have a job I could apply for.

Within a few days, Jeff responded to my email and invited me to come visit him at his company for lunch. During our meeting, he asked me lots of questions about my education and career goals. He told me about his own career journey, and how God had grown him along the way. At the end of our conversation, Jeff said something I was not expecting to hear. He said he had an open position in his department, and after our conversation he thought I'd be a good fit for it. I was flabbergasted, because the job he was offering was the exact role I was looking for.

A few months later, I eventually found out that before I had emailed Jeff, he had been praying about a role he needed to fill on his team. He didn't want to post the job because he wanted God to send him the right person. After this prayer, Jeff received an email from me mentioning things directly connected to his job opening. Unbeknownst to me, I was the answer to Jeff's prayer.

Once I learned this, I realized in a way I never had before that God was sovereignly orchestrating the events of my life. He was working in the background before I even thought about sending that email. He had allowed me to find Jeff's name and dropped in my mind the idea to email him. With strategy and intentionality, God moved me into position, as if I were a chess piece on a chessboard.

This job was not the result of a master networking plan or extensive research. There was no way for me to know that the job opening existed or that my lunch meeting was actually an informal interview. I could not have prepared the right answers because I didn't know he'd be asking me interview-type questions. All I could do was be obedient to God's leading to send an email and watch him do the rest.

Thankfully, this wasn't the last time I experienced this type of miracle in my life. There have been a few other times where God has used my obedience to do things beyond what I could have ever imagined or expected. So much so, that when people ask how it happened, I can only respond with one word—God.

With each miracle, two simple truths are ingrained deeper into my mind—*I am limited; God is not.* And each time I remember the stories, I'm reminded that my success in any season or situation does not rest solely on me, but on God. This doesn't absolve me of my responsibility to steward my situation well, but it does release me from the pressure of trying to hold onto control by myself.

While our culture's promises of self-empowerment and control are alluring, they are promises that can never be fulfilled. In the end, they don't actually lead to true peace; they compound anxiety as we worry about how to keep the plates spinning and the reins in our own hands. On our own, full control—and the promise of peace on the other side of it—will always be just beyond our reach. Any little control we have ebbs and flows based upon our ability to hold things together. Sometimes our plans work, and our research gives us the information we need to make the right decision. Over time, however, our plans start to crack. Our research becomes outdated as new information surfaces and situations we didn't anticipate pop up. We can try to keep all the plates in our life spinning on our own, but eventually we'll be too slow getting back to one plate and it will crash to the ground—along with all the peace we were trying to grasp in the first place.

God's sovereignty and omnipotence remind us that we don't have to keep the plates spinning on our own. We don't have to take on the full responsibility for navigating our lives. His control over all things in this world extends to the smallest detail. This means that the peace we desire doesn't come from trying harder or by ignoring the situation but by connecting to the One who can do what we cannot.

True, lasting, chaos-transcending peace comes from surrender as we choose to submit our heart, mind, soul, and plans to God. This creates an inextricable dependence where, like a baby in her mother's womb, we draw from an ever-flowing supply of peace. It is not one we have to cultivate or "co-collaborate with the universe" to maintain. Instead, as believers who have been reconnected to God, we receive it freely without limitation.

Habit of Resistance | Prayer

Our culture's false story of peace through control leaves us trying to hold something that will keep slipping through our hands. But God's story reminds us that we have access to a peace that will never end through surrender. To keep this peace flowing, we must loosen the grip we have on our own lives, and there's one simple but powerful habit that consistently helps us do this: prayer.

Since Jesus shows us what it looks like to live as believers, we are going to learn the significance of prayer, and all the other habits we'll discuss in this book, from him.

Learning from Jesus

Have you ever heard the phrase, *"Watch what people do, not just what they say"*? On more than one occasion, I've heard people use it as a subtle encouragement to pay attention to people's words and actions. We can learn a lot about a person—including their character, intentions, motivations, and integrity—simply by observing how they act in the world. Even when they aren't talking, a person's actions can speak very loudly.

Jesus embodied this for us during his time here on earth, as many of his teachings were validated by his actions. Specifically, we can learn a lot from Jesus's habit of being alone with God in prayer. This practice shows up in each of the Gospels. Matthew and John describe how Jesus retreated to pray after feeding the 5,000 (Matt. 14:23; John 6:15). Mark shares how Jesus spent time in prayer before he preached the

Sermon on the Mount (Mark 1:35). Luke shares how Jesus often retreated to a solitary place, especially as his ministry grew (Luke 5:16). Prayer was the way Jesus began his ministry, made important decisions, and dealt with troubling emotions like grief. It's how he dealt with the constant demands of his ministry and cared for his soul. It's how he taught his disciples. It's how he equipped for important ministry events. It's how he prepared for his death on the cross.[7]

Jesus's habit of prayer permeated the entirety of his ministry on earth. While Jesus might have been physically alone, spiritually he was communing with other persons of the Trinity. The frequency of Jesus's moments of prayer shows that he believed intimacy with his Father was vital to his ability to fulfill his divine mission. He also believed the same is true for us.

During Passover, Jesus offers his final words to his disciples before he is arrested. In this final message, he doesn't spend time giving them a typical ministry strategy. He doesn't have them create a vision board or spend time visualizing all the people they'd disciple. Rather, he tells them their success hinges on the frequency with which they spend time with God. He says, "I am the vine; you are the branches. The one who remains in me and I in him produces much fruit, because you can do nothing without me" (John 15:5).

Jesus knew what it was like to navigate life on earth. Even though he is perfectly divine and perfectly human, in his humanity, he experienced many of the struggles that are common to us. He dealt with temptation, disappointment, anger, betrayal, sadness, hunger, weariness, spiritual attacks, and many of the other difficulties that we navigate as humans living in a fallen world. Jesus knew what the disciples were up against and the difficulty of the mission he had called them to complete.

The startling part of Jesus's message in John 15:5 is the statement, "You can do nothing without me." If the disciples wondered if his call to remain in him was a command, those six words would have confirmed it. Now, by "nothing" Jesus does not mean the disciples' actions won't produce *anything* if they choose to live outside of dependence on God. Rather, their actions won't be pleasing to God; they won't complete their mission and they won't experience the abundant life he came to give them. In addition, all the goodness and peace that comes from living in God's power won't be theirs either.

With his words and actions, Jesus showed the disciples and us that intimacy with God is a nonnegotiable for those who want to navigate life well.

A Posture of Surrender

Every time we pray to God, we must remember we are responding to God's invitation to talk with him. He graciously invites us to engage in a two-way conversation where we talk and then listen to God's response. While we always need to approach God with honor and respect, our prayers don't have to be fancy. We can talk to God the same way we would talk to our friend. And like a friendship, over time, these conversations build a closeness or intimacy between us and God.

Even though prayer helps us express our concerns and needs to God, it also helps us make space to listen to him. Often our lives remain in a state of distraction and hurry.

Trapped in the current of hustle and productivity, we rarely make space to slow down and sit in silence. But it is in the silence that God speaks to our hearts, revealing things that we're not always aware of, like our pride, hurts, and fears. He will point out the sin we are trying to hide while simultaneously inviting us to confess and repent.

In our conversations with God, we are also empowered to live with a faith that believes God's plans are better than ours. He will invite us to surrender control and embrace the wisdom of the prophet Isaiah that God's ways are higher than our ways and his thoughts are higher than our thoughts (Isa. 55:8–9). As he brings his Word back to our minds, we will be reminded that his way is always better even when we don't fully understand it.

Prayer is where we receive our instructions from God and develop the battle plan we need to accomplish his divine tasks. Whether it's our undisciplined flesh or an attack from the enemy, God will show us the steps we need to take not just to survive, but to thrive. He will also provide us with encouragement that soothes our overstimulated and anxious minds, reminding us of the ways he has come through before while giving us vision for how he will show up again.

Prayer is powerful because it keeps us connected to God. We are not limitless; but when we are connected to him, we have access to his limitless character. When our control tactics of researching, planning, and "manifesting" fail, God does not. We don't have to keep the plates of our lives spinning all on our own. We also don't have to settle for what we can accomplish on our own. Prayer helps us position ourselves to receive the things that are beyond our reach, but within the reach of our boundless God. And when we give the control over to him instead of white-knuckling it for ourselves, we finally find the peace we craved all along.

Live It Out

Each chapter in this book will end with a challenge, inviting you to live out what you have just learned. For this chapter, you can now articulate the false story that is whispered all around you when it comes to peace: "The way to peace is by viewing yourself as limitless and controlling your circumstances." I want to challenge you to push against that story, breaking free from it, so you might walk in the true one: "The way to peace is by viewing yourself as limited and surrendering control to God." And the habit I want you to practice to do this? *Prayer.*

This week, set aside a time each day to pray. Open up your prayer time by writing down all the things you are worried about or the tasks you need to accomplish for that day. Then start talking to God by using the A.C.T.S. method. Begin with ADORATION, praising God for his matchless character and nature. Next, CONFESS any sin you might have committed. Then, THANK God for the ways he has previously answered your prayers, showered your life with goodness, and given you a future hope in Christ. Last, grab that sheet of paper you prepared and list out any SUPPLICATION, asking God for the things you need. Be specific and write down what you've asked for in your journal.

Close out your time in prayer thanking God for how he *will* provide for the things you need.

Friend, I encourage you to make this time of prayer a regular habit in your life. Also, when you feel the worry or anxiousness start to build, don't just assume you'll pray later. Pray immediately.[8] You don't have to wait until a special time to talk with the Lord. Throughout our day, we should have an ongoing conversation with God (1 Thess. 5:16–18). The constant communication helps us stay alert, realigns our perspective to what is true, releases our death grip on the reins, and reminds us that peace is always available to us, because the true Source of all peace is always present with us (Phil. 4:6–7).

Chapter 2

A Better Identity

I am a Black woman who grew up in predominantly White environments. Up until middle school I was one of a handful of non-white students in my school. I attended a college where out of approximately 2,000 students, fewer than 100 were Black. My experience as a minority has been complicated, with both beautiful and painful memories filling my mental scrapbook.

One of the memories that stands out is when I attended an all-white elementary school. My best friend from this portion of my childhood was (and still is) white. We were inseparable, playing for hours at my house, hers, or in the woods behind our neighborhood. One day, we went to play with some other kids who lived around the corner. She knew them better than I did, so she went up to them to ask if we could play with them. I can still see them standing a little ways in front of me, talking about me and how they didn't want to play with me because I was different. This was their way of saying they didn't want to play with me because I was Black.

This moment is frozen in my mind for many reasons, but one of them is the deep rejection I felt. Those same feelings return as I write these words. I feel for my younger self as I think of how I just wanted to be friends with these girls, but instead of friendship I was given a very clear message that I didn't belong.

Rejection is a universal experience. At one time or another, we all have been excluded from a group. It might have been some mean girls at school, an overly critical parent, or an employer who rejected your job application with the excuse, "You aren't a good fit for the team." Some of us deal with it better than others. But no matter how high of a wall we have built around our hearts, rejection still hurts. Whether or not it is intentional, people often refuse to indulge our human need for belonging.

This desire for belonging is really a desire to know who we are and how or why we have value. Our placement within a certain group often gives us answers for the following questions: *Who am I? What am I here for? Do I still matter? Am I relevant? Am I worthy or important?*

At one point or another, I think we have all asked these questions. Whether it was after a disappointing conversation, an unexpected loss, or a prolonged scrolling session on social media, we've all wondered about our identity. Some consider this selfish. However, I think our curiosity is a marker of our humanity—normal points of insecurity that pop up at different moments of our life.

Any time we whisper these questions to ourselves, we are signaling that our identity tank is empty or has at least fallen below the minimum level. This proverbial tank holds the details that help us make sense of our existence. They help us develop a sense of self-worth and understand our values and motivations. They provide direction, helping us make decisions and help us reach our purpose. A strong identity helps us not be swayed by what other people think of us and helps us bounce back when life throws an unexpected obstacle our way.

We all know what it looks like for someone to not have a strong sense of self. Their behavior is usually a little unstable as they switch identities like they do outfits, trying to find one that fits them the best. Sometimes an empty identity tank signals to them that they aren't valuable. So their behavior becomes self-destructive as they allow other people to treat them like they are worthless.

Having a strong identity is vital to our well-being. While our desire for value and meaning is interconnected with our desire for love, I believe it's different enough that it deserves its own chapter. If we all have an identity tank to fill, we need to know who gave us our tanks, why they got empty, and how to refill them.

Back to the Beginning

Have you ever noticed the amount of detail given in Genesis 1 to each part of the world God spoke into being? The pieces of nature that scientists have yet to fully understand are only given one or two lines in the Bible. Think about the complexity of the sun or the vast number of species of plants and animals that exist. A significant amount of research has been done to uncover the depths of God's creative work, with new discoveries being made all the time. But despite their beautiful complexity, the biblical text briefly mentions them and moves on.

However, there is one place the story slows down, giving us a deeper glimpse into God's creative process. In Genesis 1:26, the text lingers on the creation of humans, as we see God distinguishing humanity from the rest of creation by creating them in his image.

The placement of humanity's origins on the final day of creation is meant to be seen as a climactic moment. Said another way, God saved the best for last! We are the shining point of all creation, so beautiful that God's evaluation of his own handiwork was "very good" (Gen. 1:31)! It's worth mentioning that I said "we" for a reason, for humanity was also created together, male and female, as cohabitants of earth. This is significant because our sense of belonging is connected to our relationship with God and with others.

The word for "image" in Genesis 1:26–27 is *tselem*, which refers to the idols or statues of gods that would be placed in their respective temples. This was a common practice by ancient Near Eastern peoples like the Babylonians and Egyptians. In her book *Being God's Image*, Carmen Imes shares that "the people of the ancient Near East associated creation with temples and temples with gardens."[1]

The people of the ancient Near East had a culture vastly different from ours, so a bit of context will help us understand why this additional detail about the word "image" is important. Let's look at the following quote from Imes. I believe it will help us uncover the implications of us being images of God placed in his earthly temple.

> Could it be that the Israelite temple lacks a Yahweh idol because God has already placed an image in his cosmic temple? Just as a statue of a god is intended to represent that god's claim to a particular area, so humans are the physical representation of the creator God on earth. And just as an idol is meant to deflect praise to the actual deity, so humans are to deflect praise to Yahweh. . . . We need to view the *imago Dei* as a declaration that God intended to create human persons to be the physical means through which he would manifest his own divine presence in the world. God is not usually visible, so he appoints humans to remind creation and each other of his presence.[2]

As idols in God's divine earthly temple, you and I were created to worship God and serve as a reminder to all of creation to worship him. We do this through our fulfillment of the commands God gave to us in Genesis 1:28, "Be fruitful, multiply, fill the earth, and subdue it. Rule the fish of the sea, the birds of the sky, and every creature that crawls on the earth." Specifically, the words *subdue* and *rule* point to how we are to care for all that God has created. We are stewards who, with all our unique gifts and personalities, have been tasked with the responsibility to care for God's world in the same benevolent way he would.

Our identity is directly tied to God. We belong to him, and it is from this connection that we derive our value and sense of purpose. We only make sense when we are connected to him. Outside of this connection, we take on the impossible responsibility of figuring out who we are. Furthermore, since we were created to be worshippers, reflecting the glory of whomever we worship, our efforts to find identity will inevitably leave us looking for another god to represent.

Our Culture's Story: *An Earned Identity*

In our search for identity, we tend to gravitate toward groups that connect with some aspect of who we are. These groups, communities, or tribes, offer a gathering space where we can meet other people like us and gain vision for how to live in this world through the lens of our shared interests and beliefs. They give us structure around how we spend our money, time, and interact with the people around us.

For example, if you are a huge sports fan, then much of your life will revolve around your favorite sports team(s). Over time, you will learn the stats for your favorite players and teams. These details or "holy book verses" will help you connect to other sports enthusiasts as you talk about them in "small group" conversations with one another. You will learn more about your teams by listening to "preachers and teachers" on sports radio or sports commentary TV shows.

To help show your support for your team you might use or "tithe" your money to buy tickets to a game, spend hours getting in and out of the stadium, and even travel to different cities to see the team play at these "church services." Or you will just attend "virtual church" by watching the game from home. For those who are the most engaged, their die-hard commitment will be made evident through the jerseys, T-shirts, face paint, and other "religious garments and adornments" they wear to show their allegiance to their sports "god."

Now, before you throw away this book or put it down to write me an email to share how upset you are with me, please know this sports illustration is meant to be a little spicy and satirical! A healthy engagement with sports is not sinful, rather it is a great way to have fun and meet like-minded people. My goal with the illustration is to help you see the ways we are wired to worship as we grow to reflect the interests of whichever god we decide to follow. Contrary to what nonbelievers might say, Christians aren't weird. Everyone worships someone or something, the only difference is that Christians worship the one true God.

We are familiar with many of the communities our culture invites us to join to find identity, like our sexuality, race, positions of prestige in the workplace, or political affiliation. However, if those weren't enough, here are a few other groups that have open enrollment in digital spaces:

The Beauty Group

This group affirms that value and meaning is attached to beauty, and those who rate higher on the beauty scale will be more celebrated and loved. Entrance comes through adherence to our culture's beauty standards, which can be found through the most frequently shared and liked pictures online. Long hair, skinny bodies, chiseled faces, lifted backsides, and youthful skin are the epitome of beauty in America. So those who want to participate in this group will have habits that help them achieve these outcomes. This includes procedures that will permanently alter our bodies, like Botox, Brazilian butt lifts (BBLs), face lifts, breast implants, liposuction, nose jobs, and other forms of plastic surgery. We will also follow strict nutrition plans and gym regimens to help us sculpt and maintain our bodies.

To learn the ways of this group, we will religiously watch tutorials from the sea of beauty and fashion influencers who will guide us in the worship of our appearance. At their recommendation, we will amass closets and drawers full of makeup products, clothes, shoes, and jewelry. More than we could ever possibly use or wear.

The Wellness Group

This group affirms that value and meaning are connected to a positive life—meaning, a life devoid of any mental and emotional pain (or even discomfort). Entrance comes through the realization that you aren't happy. But you don't need to go to a licensed medical professional to find out why. Instead, you can get your answer from an online wellness influencer. As you scroll through their videos, simply find what you resonate with the most. It could be a "self-diagnosis" of PTSD, narcissistic personality disorder, or attachment styles.[3] It could also be words and phrases like "triggering," "love bombing," or "my spouse stopped meeting my needs." Again, no need to get confirmation or advice from a doctor, pastor, counselor, or psychologist—just go with your gut.

Once you have your self-given explanation or diagnosis, you need to come up with a healing plan. To do this, continue to consume information from wellness influencers. Participate in their retreats, buy their books, listen to their podcasts, and sign up for their life coaching programs. They will help you "lock in" and focus on what matters most: your journey to positivity.

Last, you must train your community to be supportive. If they aren't, you need to remove them from your life because they stand between you and your healing. When asked why you are distancing yourself from them, tell them you are "protecting your peace" or that you are getting rid of relationships that no longer serve you. Eventually, your community will only contain people on your level who support your wellness journey without question.

The Productivity Group

This group affirms that value and meaning are found in what we produce. The more we do, the more value and meaning we have. Therefore, entrance into the productivity group comes through getting more done. It could be a clothing line, stationery, social media content, or a real estate firm. The quantity of your production matters more than what you produce. This might mean you don't get to see your family or friends as much as you would like. But to produce, you have to work.

Content creation is a huge part of this group's habits. Others must see what you are doing. Share about the lifestyle you can afford with your income, like a car, home, or luxury vacation. You will need to share about your business process as well. Show people the long nights, early mornings, victories, and a few failures that have all led to your success.

To learn the ways of this group, you need to learn from productivity gurus. They will help you get started, recommend the right systems and mindset habits you need so you can meet your goals and even turn your 5-to-9 into your 9-to-5. You will buy their books, listen to their podcasts, purchase their master classes, and invest in their coaching programs. You'll also need to surround yourself with other like-minded people, because they are the only ones who understand the sacrifices you need to make to be a top producer.

The Influencer Group (a.k.a. The Power Group)

This group affirms that value and meaning are found by having power over other people. Entrance into this group comes through you having a following, the bigger the better. People can follow you for any reason. You might influence how they vote, what they buy, or what they think about Jesus. Or your influence might come through economic means, as your wealth gives you increased access to opportunities and privileges that are unavailable to most people.

However, your goal isn't to serve anyone's interests but your own. You must amass and hold onto your influence and power by any means necessary. This might come through strategic content creation where you twist the truth just a bit to make your content more persuasive. Post plenty of pictures of you with other powerful people—this will give you prestige and more followers. When people start to question your views, don't engage them. Shame and block them. Don't leave space for dissenters. (If your place of power is somewhere outside of digital spaces, for example, in your business, this looks like micromanaging your employees, creating a culture of fear, and exaggerating your success so people won't notice any of your failures.)

Formed by Culture

Again, please don't throw this book in the trash. There can be good things found in each of these areas of interest for people. For example, there is nothing wrong with buying makeup, having a positive attitude, or working hard. But I described these groups in an exhaustive (and satirical) way to illustrate how far we can go when we root or anchor our identity in their way of living. I could have easily listed off a plethora of other communities or tribes that provide us with the same opportunity. As varied as our personalities are, is as varied as the opportunities we have to find value and belonging outside of God.

Ultimately, to hold our spot in the group and receive all its benefits one thing is required: our loyalty and allegiance. Our decisions must be driven by the values and beliefs of the group. This means that how we spend our time, our money, and how we treat other people will all be determined by the group. And when the values of the Bible conflict with these values, we end up choosing the identity we find in the group over the identity we find in God.

Sadly, left unchecked, these groups turn us into slaves whose sense of self is fragile. Our identity will fluctuate based upon how much or how little we do. Since our identity is earned through our achievements, it fluctuates based upon how much or how little we do and it is our responsibility to maintain the necessary standards or "membership requirements." Whenever we are unable to meet the requirements, our identity—sense of value, purpose, privilege, or power—fades away. Simply put, we lose our spot in the group.

When we are chasing identities we have to earn through achievement, our lives become beholden to the group and the gods they lead us to worship, gods who appear benevolent but are ruthless taskmasters in disguise.

If we stop adhering to Western beauty standards, we lose our spot. If we stop producing at levels that are notable, we lose our spot. If we don't ruthlessly remove "toxic" people from our life, we lose our spot. If we lose our ability to influence other people, we lose our spot.

Sadly, these groups don't care about what their demands will cost us—mentally, relationally, physically, and emotionally. Only by abiding by these groups' commands will we receive the benefits they promise.

God's Story: *A Given Identity*

The Ten Commandments are a passage familiar to nonbelievers and believers alike. You may have learned them as a child in Sunday school or seen them on the wall of your grade school classroom. Many of us see them as a list of rules that Israel had to follow to be in relationship with God. If they checked all the boxes off the list, then they would go to heaven. While this is an understandable perspective, it's not entirely accurate.

Given to Israel in Exodus 20, the Ten Commandments were part of a bigger set of instructions called the Law. At this point in the biblical story, God had just delivered Israel out of slavery. After this amazing display of both his power and his commitment to Israel, God invites them to enter into a relationship agreement with him called a covenant. In this covenant, God commits to be their God, and Israel pledges that they will belong to him as his people. This is not the first time he has done this with Israel. God made a covenant with their forefather Abraham in Genesis, so this is a reaffirmation of the commitments he has previously made.

God's presentation of the Ten Commandments to Israel begins with an important reminder. In Exodus 20:2–3 God says, "I am the LORD your God, who brought you out of the land of Egypt, out of the place of slavery. Do not have other gods besides me." Before God lays out the stipulations of his agreement with Israel, making clear his expectations for how they are to love one another and love him, he reminds them of how he delivered them from slavery. These introductory words are a reminder that God's love and grace for Israel preceded their obedience. Israel would not earn a spot in the group of God's people through their obedience, rather their obedience was meant to be an act of gratitude for what was already theirs.[4]

Up until this point in the Bible, God had already acted on their behalf numerous times. Through Moses, he had already made provisions for them that affirmed their personhood, value, and belonging with him. Through the Ten Commandments God is not dangling a carrot in front of them, asking them to perform certain actions to get the prize of a spot as a part of his family. Rather, he is inviting them to a way of living that will help them experience the fullness of *who they already are*—of what has always been and will always be true of them as image-bearers.

Even though Israel will struggle to live in obedience to this way of life, God still chooses to bear the responsibility to reestablish them as his people (Jer. 31:31–34). Again, their participation in the group is not based upon their efforts but God's grace.

Throughout the rest of the Old Testament, Israel will be invited to affirm their status as God's people through their adherence to the law. They will come to delight in the law, seeing it as the lamp that lights their way (Ps. 119:105). Rather than a burden, the law will be seen as a tool that helps order the lives of God's people, both individually and corporately. It will teach them how to love God and love one another. In books like Psalms, Proverbs, and Ecclesiastes, adhering to

God's law will be compared to walking in the way of wisdom, with disobedience likened to walking in the way of folly.

But as these passages of law are tucked into the storyline of the Bible, so too are numerous examples of God pursuing Israel, delivering Israel, sustaining, protecting, healing, and providing an outpouring of his grace. From the very beginning God was committed to his creation, desiring for them to live out their divine design as his image-bearers. He fulfills this commitment emphatically through Christ. Instead of being fragile, their spot in the group was steady and sure—not because they earned it, but because God graciously declared it to be so.

Formed by God

A friend of mine has several children, two of whom are adopted. Their adoption journey began as fostering. Eventually, it became apparent that these two kiddos would be a good fit for their family, and they began the journey to adopt them. Adoption gave them a permanent spot in their family, and this new identity was formalized when the kids took the last name of their new family unit.

Anyone you talk to about fostering and adoption will tell you it's a beautifully hard process. Sometimes foster children come from unhealthy environments that have left their mark on the kids. Working through this trauma can be difficult and taxing as the path to healing is usually long and slow. This proved to be true for my friend, as her newly adopted children brought deep wounds with them into their new family. These wounds manifested through patterns of behavior that were destructive, both to the child and the family as a whole.

However, instead of giving up, my friend leaned in. These were her kids, and she was going to do everything in her power to help them flourish. Through counseling, special school programs, tough love, patience, and lots of prayer, my friend and her husband have fought to help her kids find healing. She did this out of love, and because she never wanted them to question their space in the family or their value compared to the rest of the biological children. They were family, no matter what.

There's something unique about being a member of a family unit. When it's healthy, it provides you a place of identity that never moves, no matter what you do. You might put tension on the relationship, making family dinners a bit awkward, but you are still invited to the table. There is always a seat for you.

The surety of this position affects your identity and actions. Again, in healthy families, you live without the possibility that your seat might be revoked. This produces a confidence and freedom that feels safe, but that also calls you higher. The family bond produces within you a desire to honor those around the table, to have a life they can be proud of because it reflects everyone's shared values.

As believers, the grace of God adopts us into a family (Rom. 8:15; Eph. 1:5; Gal. 4:5). It gives us a permanent seat at a table where we are always welcome and loved. When life is going well, we have a seat. When our lives get too friendly with sin, we still have a seat. Now, in those seasons the conversation around the table might be a little tense. But, no matter what we do, our position in the family can never be revoked. We are given a permanent space in an environment that will shape us to be who we were intended to be as image-bearers.

This grace we receive from God should not leave us unchanged. Rather, it produces a confidence that helps us rest. No longer are we driven by the need to achieve our value or sense of purpose. Instead, we live freely *from* it. We live like children who, regardless of our appearance, successes or failures, or level of influence, know we are always welcome. Out of gratitude, we arrange our decisions and motivations to fit the shared values of this family. The grace of God leads us to want to honor the One who through Christ made space for us.

What identities are being thrown at you all day long? What spaces of belonging are tempting you to think you have to earn your spot? In the end, we don't need those thousands of other identities, for we already have an eternal identity in God's household that can never be shaken. As Ephesians 2:19 says, "You are no longer foreigners and strangers" to the beloved people of God, "but fellow citizens with the saints, and members of God's household." More than even members of his general household, we are God's eternal *children*, as Romans 8:16 and 1 John 3:1–2 declare over us. This means that no matter what other earthly "hat" we temporarily wear, being God's child is the heavenly identity that stands the test of time. We're safe. We belong. We have an identity that we cannot lose. Praise be to the God who led us out of the slavery of earning our place and into a seat at his family table that cannot be taken from us!

Habit of Resistance | The (Spiritual Family) Gathering

Our culture's false story about identity leaves us trying to earn our value and a spot of belonging by adhering to the standards of our affinity group of choice. But these standards are fluid, changing without notice, and if we fail to meet them we have to give up our seat at the table. Thankfully, God's story reminds us that we have inherent value and identity because we are created in his image and have been adopted into his family. Our spot at God's table is secure, no matter what we do we will always belong with God and his people. To remind us of this, there is one place we need to regularly show up to and participate in: our (spiritual) family gathering.

Learning from Jesus

One of the cultural dynamics in Scripture that can get missed by those of us in Western American culture is collectivism. Both in the Old and New Testament, people understood their sense of identity, purpose, and belonging based upon the group they were a part of—most likely their family of origin.[5] These deep ties of kinship would be accompanied by deep responsibilities to care for and seek the interest of one's family members.

Several times in the Gospels, Jesus takes this cultural dynamic and flips it, showing that the family he was most tied to was not biological but spiritual. In Luke 8:21, after being told that his mother and brothers were waiting to see him, Jesus says, "My mother and my brothers are those who hear and do the word of God." A few chapters later in Luke 11:27, Jesus is teaching the crowds and a woman yells out, "Blessed is the womb that bore you and the one who nursed you!" Jesus replies, "Rather, blessed are those who hear the word of God and keep it" (v. 28). Moreover in Luke 14:26, Jesus teaches that discipleship requires believers to find identity in the family of God before what is for many of us our most precious identity—our nuclear family.

In all of these passages, it's clear that Christ is showing that life in the kingdom of God is lived as part of a new family. The values, purpose, and rooted place of belonging that was once determined by our biological family is now determined by our spiritual family. This includes both responsibility and privileges, as we are to care for one another and receive care as well. These kinship ties are affirmed all throughout the New Testament, as the word used the most to describe believers is not "Christian" but *adelphoi*, meaning "brothers and sisters."[6] This language makes clear that we are to relate to one another as dear family members, as together we help to push forward Christ's kingdom mission in this world.

However, alongside this new family reality, Christ is not just affirming how we are to identify with one another but that he identifies with us. Think about it, in these Luke passages Christ repeatedly emphasizes how he would rather identify with us, his spiritual family, over and against all other available identities offered to him! Jesus Christ, the Son of God and our elder brother in his Father's household, chooses to ultimately identify with you and me as his adopted sisters and brothers! He has not left us at the kids table while he sits at another one.

He also does not make us earn a seat at his table. Instead, he graciously sits alongside us, communes with us, and will feast with us when he returns (Rev. 19:6–9)!

A Seat at the Table

Historically, Christians have come together at our "family gathering" also known as church. In the days of the early church, this gathering included the things we see listed in Acts 2:42–47, like biblical teaching and prayer. But it also included the Lord's Supper which, instead of our wafer and cup of grape juice, was a full meal.[7] When believers met together, it provided a time for them to rehearse the truths that anchored their faith, pray corporately, baptize new believers, and then break bread together to remember Christ's sacrifice as they waited for him to return.

However, this gathering was not the only time believers saw one another. They often lived near each other geographically, so there were opportunities to meet, serve one another, and be encouraged throughout the week. Each time believers came together in these close-knit communities, they "devoted themselves to the apostles' teaching, to fellowship, to the breaking of bread, and to prayer" (Acts 2:42). In doing so, they reaffirmed their corporate identity as followers of Jesus whose value and purpose was inherently tied to God. It was a time characterized by hospitality, humility, service, and generosity.

Some things have not changed since then. Each time we show up to our spiritual family gathering, we strengthen our ability to resist the pull of our culture. Our time together helps us remember who we really are. When together, we affirm our identity in the way we treat one another and challenge each other to treat the world. For some of us, our time with our brothers and sisters in the faith resembles these first gatherings of Christians. But, for a growing number of us, they look more like a concert or event you attend than a group of people you do life with.

On one hand, the production level of some church services is top notch. With worship that feels like a concert and preaching that is so dynamic, clips of the sermons go viral online. But we enter and exit these event venues as strangers, disconnected from the people around us. This disconnection robs us of the blessing of experiencing life with our spiritual family. It robs us of the reminders of our value that come from spiritual brothers and sisters who by word and deed affirm your identity in Christ. It robs you of the accountability they provide when you are not living up to that identity. It also robs you of having a secure seat at the family table, because when your presence doesn't matter you will give up your seat to find another seat at our culture's table where it does matter.

Church is not just about a program. It's supposed to be a gathering space of disciples who grow together, encouraging one another to live out their shared values and beliefs. When we are beaten down by the world and discouraged by the difficulties of life, we are able to come together with our family to be reminded of what really matters. We are challenged in our faith, supported in our struggles, and celebrated when our prayers are answered by God. Our spiritual family reminds us that the work we do, whether it's as a business owner, educator, doctor, or tradesman, is to help restore shalom. We push back the darkness and bring the light of Christ everywhere we go. We recognize our greatest ministry is not simply within the wall of the family house, but outside the house as we share the gospel in word and deed with those around us.

At the family gathering, we help shield one another's eyes from the blinding lights of the world's temptations as we remind each other that we have value and meaning because our lives are rooted in and lived in service to God.

Live It Out

Our culture's false story sounds like this: "Your identity, value, and belonging must be earned. As long as you keep doing what your affinity group requires, you keep your spot. Once you stop performing, you'll lose it." But God's gospel story offers us another option: "Your identity, value, and place of belonging are given to you by God. You don't have to earn them and they will never be revoked." The habit of the family gathering at our local church (e.g., Sunday service) provides us with a weekly reminder of this truth. Sometimes, this reminder is more frequent as we have additional opportunities to be around our spiritual family through small groups and other ministry events. Especially in seasons of brokenness or hardship, these regular touch points provide the support we need to keep moving forward.

I'll be honest, though, while the habit of attending the family gathering is valuable, it is not always easy. It takes time to build relationships with people and issues of church hurt can make it difficult to persevere in community. However, I encourage you to continue leaning in, even when it's hard. A part of our faith journey is trusting that in the moments we can't clearly see what God is doing, our obedience to his direction produces things within and through us that are for our good and God's glory. So keep showing up and finding opportunities to participate in your local family gathering until God tells you otherwise.

To help you apply what you learned in this chapter, I want to challenge you to lean into your family of God identity with the same intentionality you give to the other "groups" you are involved in. Specifically, I want you to build habits to get involved in God's household as your *primary* identity. It's one thing to *say* that being God's child and a member of God's household is your primary identity. It's another thing entirely to practice consistent habits that get you involved in that household more often than you are involved in other identifying groups.

Take some time this week to reflect on what this might look like for you and start by considering the habits you practice with the other groups you are involved with, both online and offline. Maybe you could redirect some of your purchasing fund to support the family gathering. Instead of buying a new beauty product, outfit, or tech gadget, you, a "family member" could contribute additional funds (i.e., tithes) to the "family fund" to help support the needs of the family while they move forward in their kingdom mission. Instead of attending a local meetup with your running club or an online productivity master class, make time to attend or lead a small group. Or when you are feeling disconnected and lonely, instead of scrolling mindlessly, cook a meal for one of your family members who is in need and drop it off at their house.

As believers, we need to be involved in the community, being a light for Christ in our city and neighborhoods. However, sometimes we can have more involvement in groups outside of the church than we do the family of God. The more intentional we are about ordering our lives around our spiritual family, the greater opportunities we have to experience the unending blessing of identity, purpose, and belonging it brings our way.

Chapter 3

A Better Love

What song comes to mind for you when you think about love? For me, it's Tina Turner's "What's Love Got to Do with It." At the 1985 Grammy Awards, it won Song of the Year, Record of the Year, and Best Female Pop Vocal Performance. In 2012, it was inducted into the Grammy Hall of Fame. Needless to say, this song was a hit both in America and across the world.

When it starts to play, you hear a sultry pop and R&B vibe that makes you think Tina is going to sing about a deep and affectionate relationship that has stood the test of time. However, when you start to listen to the lyrics, you quickly realize she is telling a different story.

When she refers to love as a second-hand emotion, or asks why anyone would involve their own heart in a relationship when hearts can easily be broken, it becomes apparent that there is no desire to invest, pour into, serve, or even open herself to receive love from the person she is with. What is valuable to her in this relationship is what she gets from the other person. But with over 515 million streams on Spotify, her perspective clearly resonates with a lot of people. While love is something so many desire, we don't have an easy time finding it.

In our quest to find love, many of us are chasing an emotion. We are searching for a feeling that comes and goes depending on the day or the experience you have with a person. When I think about this type of "love," I picture a couple in the honeymoon phase of their relationship. If you've ever seen one of these couples out on a date or remember when you were in this stage of a relationship, you know that the feelings of love are very evident.

Between the displays of affection, their physical closeness, or prolonged eye-contact, these couples seem to have a love that places them in a bubble. They are the only two people in the world who seem to exist. As you sink deeper and deeper into this emotional connection, you are more willing to be honest about who you are because you feel as if the person you are connected to will never leave you. In that moment, it's hard to imagine they would do anything but accept you for who you are.

Moreover, we believe this romantic feeling is driven by what someone does for us. Gary Chapman captures this dynamic in his book *The 5 Love Languages*, where he describes five main ways we receive love—words of affirmation, quality time, receiving gifts, acts of service, and physical touch. While we can feel loved through all the love languages, each of us has one that is at the top of their "this is how you love me well" list.

Having someone show you love using your primary love language is powerful. While most of us appreciate any kind gesture of affection, experiencing our top love language makes it feel like the other person really knows you or "sees" you. Whether the relationship is romantic or not, this type of love allows us to experience intimacy and the privilege of belonging without shame.

Back to the Beginning

When I come across a verse that seems a bit odd, I find myself asking, "Why was *this* verse included in this passage?" Sometimes at first glance the verse looks out of place, providing information or details that could have been left to the reader's imagination. Genesis 2:25 is one of these verses for me. After God forms Eve out of Adam's rib and the two become one, "Both the man and his wife were naked, yet felt no shame."

At this point I began thinking, *Did you have to tell us Adam and Eve were naked? I think we know what happens when two become one.* But since the Bible is written with an economy of words, every detail is important. So I quickly got over myself and started to look closely at the passage to see why the author included this detail in the story. The significance of this verse comes to light only a few verses later. In Genesis 3:7 we are told, "The eyes of both of them were opened and they knew they were naked; so they sewed fig leaves together and made coverings for themselves."

Why did Adam and Eve suddenly decide to cover up? They felt shame.

Before sin, Adam and Eve felt known and unhindered in the most vulnerable version of themselves. But, after sinning, Adam and Eve are ashamed, hiding from God, and blaming each other for their foolish decisions. Shame is not always a bad thing. Sometimes it is a helpful tool that brings us back into right behavior.[1] But the shame we see Adam and Eve experience in Genesis 3 is a fissure, a permanent shift in their relationship with God and one another that they are unable to repair.

This tragic moment feels like a significant shift for Adam and Eve and for humanity. It's a strong contrast between the life we were created to have and where Adam and Eve found themselves. We were designed to live without shame. Adam and Eve's pre-fall relationship shows us they inhabited a place of belonging that provided safety for the most vulnerable pieces of their personhood. But this place of belonging points to something greater: God created humanity with an overflow of love, and he designed our environment for us to connect with him and one another.

When the perfect relationship between God and humanity was damaged, our closeness with God began to dry up. Immediately Adam and Eve found themselves looking for a way to remedy their situation, using fig leaves to try to hide their shame. As their sons and daughters, we too are searching for the place of belonging we once had. But what we long for isn't what we always experience because we get confused about one small detail—true love doesn't always *feel* good.

Our Culture's Story: *A Blind Love*

Some phrases in our culture like, *be the change [you wish to see in the world],* or *trust the process,* are repeated so much they become a part of our American vernacular. People regularly share them online as motivational posts or repeat them to themselves as affirmations. When it comes to the topic of love, one phrase rises to the top of the motivational quote list—*follow your heart.*

The hope behind "following your heart" is genuinely sweet and idyllic, the kind that reminds you of your favorite Disney movie. It communicates the simple idea that whenever we find ourselves lost in a dark cloud of confusion, our hearts will light the way home. Whatever our hearts feel serves as a beacon, signaling which direction we should move. When the feelings are positive, we move forward, when they are negative, we move away. The hope is that in our relationships, our hearts will lead us to a place of true love, belonging, and safety.

We love following our hearts. Consider, for instance, the proliferation of relationship shows like *Love Is Blind.* This show is a social experiment that considers whether you can fall in love with someone without seeing them physically. Contestants spend time talking to each other one-on-one in "pods." These small rooms are separated by a screen, so while they can hear each other they cannot see each other. It is only once they have chosen someone—and proposed to them—that they are able to see each other in person.

Through creative storytelling, producers pull us into the fairy tale. During each episode, the viewers watch the contestants go on dates in these pods. They spend hours getting to know each other, all without seeing them. We also hear from contestants on their own in confessional scenes. I'll admit, these are my favorite parts of reality TV shows, as contestants tend to be more honest when it's just them, the producers, and the camera. Week after week, we hear stories about how they are finding love or finding duds, as they process through their experience in the pods. We are invited to believe the social experiment is genuine, as real people are looking for real love with only their hearts to guide them.

However, the hearts of the contestants tend to lead them in the direction that contains fiery passion, infatuation, and deep emotional intimacy. In the process, many ignore "red flags." Anger issues, narcissistic behavior, emotional immaturity, and selfishness often get overlooked because the feelings of "love" are so strong. With each episode, the contestants' hearts tell them to move forward, while those of us watching are screaming at the TV for them to move back.

By the time we reach the reunion episode, it becomes painfully apparent that these social experiments tend not to end well as most of the couples who get together don't stay together. Eventually, each relationship is invaded by the difficulty of life or the brokenness of the contestants. Unfortunately, for many, the light of their good feelings of love gets snuffed out. Instead of leaning in to do the necessary work to heal the relationship or oneself, people shift blame and move on.

Although following their heart got them into this predicament, contestants are never invited to question the skill set of their "guide." Instead, they are encouraged to continue following it out the door of the relationship, as their heart tells them an absence of good feelings means it's time to leave. At the end of the reunion, these contestants summarize their broken relationship with a final word in which they frequently mention that they are still hoping to find love.

It can be easy to judge the contestants of shows like *Love Is Blind*. With our armchair commentary, we complain about the contestant's inability to see the error of their relationship habits. But even though this dynamic is magnified on relationships shows, we have been guilty of doing the same thing. At one time or another, most of us have "followed our hearts." Driven by the good feelings of love, we have jumped headfirst into a relationship and ignored the warning signs. Then we have backed away from these relationships when things inevitably got hard, choosing a fresh start over the work of rebuilding.

Formed by Culture

While "following our hearts" to good feelings may seem harmless, it is driven by self-indulgence. Slowly, over time, this guide teaches us to value relational dynamics that give us dopamine hits of infatuation or deep affection. Simultaneously, it teaches us to make our way to the door when the "good feelings" stop. So, while we desire to find relationships where we can know and be known deeply, our guide causes us to self-sabotage. Ultimately, what is required for deep relationships goes against the training our self-indulgent hearts have given us.

Now, I am not saying we should ignore our emotions, nor am I saying that our feelings are not important pieces of any decision-making process. Our emotions are God-given, which means they are beautiful. Embracing them, understanding them, and processing them in healthy ways is essential to our spiritual maturity. However, the guide we use to interpret them will either lead us to a place of spiritual health or leave us spiritually unhealthy.

True belonging requires selflessness. But, simply put, by encouraging us to follow a guide that prioritizes self, our culture is forming us to be selfish. We are being trained to consider what we can receive over what we can give or what love requires of us. Our posture in relationships is to first look for ways we can experience love, rather than how we can give it to others.

At this point you might be thinking, *Wow, Elizabeth. That's a little harsh. Selfish? Really?*

I'll admit, anytime someone uses the word *selfish*, the person they are talking about is rarely painted in a good light. Being described as selfish is almost never positive. But what if we saw "selfish" as less of a valuation of our personhood and more of a description of our lack of vision? When we are primarily focused on receiving from others, our view of ourselves—specifically our "giving capacity"—is distorted.

The relationships that we want, ones with vulnerability and safety, require a certain level of emotional and spiritual maturity to exist. To engage in these relationships, we have to be people who are willing to be honest, while extending grace for people's imperfections. We have to be willing to be courageous, inviting people to build friendships with us and being resilient when in one way or another they say no. We have to be willing to confess and repent when we are wrong, owning our shortcomings but not allowing them to define us. We have to be willing to embrace the hard pieces of our story that make it difficult for us to love others freely.

Flourishing relationships require us to lean in, doing work that is often uncomfortable and hard. But when we only see our needs and not the needs of the other person, we won't know how or why to lean in. This blind spot is the reason we see people who hold us accountable as toxic or embrace the expectation that love requires people to accept us as we are. It's the reason we use "good vibes only" as the standard friendships must meet to stay in existence and the reason we choose to "protect our peace" when the good vibes start to go away.

The truth is that some friendships and relationships simply don't work. Sometimes it's because our personalities clash or different lifestyles make it difficult to be together. Many friendships only last for a season. Often, we only have a small group of friends that goes the distance with us. Our other friends may have a prominent space in our lives for a season and when the seasons change, their presence is not as prominent. But with these relationships, the hope is that we still give and share love, regardless of the length of the season.

Under our culture's tutelage, we slowly become people who struggle to cultivate flourishing relationships. Blindly following the guide of self-indulgence erodes our capacity for commitment and our desire to do the work that makes relationships thrive. Left unchecked, our "love blind spot" will produce transactional relationships that have shorter timetables, less depth, or that fail to materialize at all. We will develop a short emotional muscle memory that leads us to stop loving others well when they stop being useful to us.

You can see glimmers of this in our generation's struggle with loneliness. It is so significant that the Surgeon General declared it to be a national epidemic in 2023. We are the most connected generation, yet so many of us feel disconnected, with lives devoid of the vulnerability and safety we crave.

Like any problem that affects millions of people, the reasons for our shared experience of loneliness are layered and complex. Knowing how to navigate relationships is hard and many of us have picked up wounds over the years from people who did not love us well. However, I wonder how much of our lack is rooted in our corporate blind spot. Are we so focused on what we need other people to do for us—or how we expect them to make us feel twenty-four hours a day—that we fail to see that what we desire is right in front of us?

God's Story: *A Committed Love*

As we turn the pages of the Bible, we continue to see how God remains committed to his people. With an intentional redundancy, the biblical authors tell us that *God is with* his people: with Abraham, with Moses, with Esther, with David, with Isaiah and Jeremiah, with Mary, with Peter, with Lydia, Phoebe, and a host of others too numerous to name.[2] While to our human minds this consistent "with-ness" might seem surprising, it shouldn't be. God's gracious and persevering companionship is not simply a benevolent gesture; rather, it is the overflow of his unchanging character.

The word that is used to describe this divine attribute is *hesed*. Translated as "lovingkindness," "faithfulness," and "covenant love," *hesed* points to a loyal, selfless love that motivates a person to do voluntarily what no one has a right to expect or ask of them.[3] The first time God describes himself to his people, this is the word he uses. In Exodus 34:6, as he passes before Moses, he proclaims this about his own character: "The Lord—the Lord is a compassionate and gracious God, slow to anger and abounding in *faithful love* and truth." Faithful love is *hesed*.

God's faithful love is affection that is made apparent through consistent action. God genuinely delights in his creation. The Psalms help to remind us of this truth as over and over they proclaim how God's faithful love for his people reaches to heaven (Pss. 36:5; 57:10; 103:11; 108:4). When I look up toward the heavens, the space between it and earth seems limitless. So when the psalmist uses this measure to describe how much God loves us, he is helping us embrace the weighty truth that God's *hesed* has no limits. His relational commitment is unending, as he continues to show up for his people even when we are undeserving of his gracious love and care. "I have loved you with an everlasting love," God says (Jer. 31:3). And he means it.

Page after page in Scripture is full of examples of God's *hesed* love; moreover, it shows him being faithful to a people who were not faithful to him. It is his faithful love that leads him to deliver Israel out of slavery, provide manna for them in the wilderness, and act mercifully when they decide to create and worship a golden calf because they were tired of waiting for Moses to come back.

God's faithful love leads him to adjust his plans for Israel rather than abandon them when they get too scared to enter the Promised Land. God's faithful love is patient and waits forty years to make good on a promise he gave hundreds of years prior to Abraham. It gives Israel victory after victory in the Promised Land of Canaan and during the period of the judges, God's faithful love provides deliverance for Israel, even as their faithfulness toward him deteriorates into total forgetfulness.

God's faithful love doesn't always result in a life of comfort and ease though. God's discipline of his people in the splintering of Israel's kingdom and their exile into Babylon isn't something that brought them warm fuzzies. However, even when it's a tough love, God's *hesed* is always moving toward his goal of restoration as promised in Genesis 3:15. God created a human society in which his children enjoy perfect fellowship with each other, the created world, and the Creator.[4] Sin has corrupted this reality and God is on a mission to restore it. His *hesed* love is working to bring humanity back into relationship with him, because it is the only place they will flourish and thrive.

Formed by God

Every so often, I find myself being courageous enough to jump into the dating pool. One of these moments was a few months ago, when I met a really nice guy at an event. We had a good connection, so I decided to be the modern woman and reach out to initiate a time to hang out. Honestly, I was proud of myself. I stepped out of my comfort zone and ended up successfully making plans to meet. He even suggested a great restaurant for us to try! Winning!

Since I'm sharing this story, you are probably thinking, *Elizabeth, what's the catch? What happened?!* Well, nothing happened, because, several months later, I'm still waiting for him to respond to my "are you still good to meet up" text. In short, he ghosted me.

If you have never had the privilege of being ghosted, it is when someone you know stops communicating without notice. You might have met them on a dating app, or they could be a boyfriend/girlfriend, friend, or family member. What may have begun as a cordial conversation is stopped short when they don't respond for weeks, months, years, or ever. Without explanation, whoever you were talking to has abruptly abandoned the relationship and seemingly dropped off the face of the earth.

Even though it seems harsh, ghosting is a pretty common practice. But while so many of us have normalized this behavior, there is one who I am glad doesn't practice this toxic habit—God.

As I write this, I am getting a little teary thinking about how healing God's love is. People will abandon you for any small infraction—or as it is with ghosting, for no infraction at all. But God's love is never absent, and it is always working for our good. As Romans 5:5 teaches us, the Spirit is always pouring the faithful love of God into our hearts. What makes this even more beautiful, however, is that this pouring doesn't stop its flow with us. It flows *through* us. The experience of the unconditional and unlimited love of God compels us to become the type of people who share the same love we've been given. I love how Carolyn Custis James describes how God's *hesed* should form us:

> [Hebrew scholars] tell us *hesed* is a strong Hebrew word that sums up the ideal lifestyle for God's people. It's the way God intended for human beings to live together from the beginning—the "love-your-neighbor-as-yourself" brand of living, an active, selfless, sacrificial caring for one another that goes against the grain of our fallen natures. . . . It's actually the kind of love we find most fully expressed in Jesus. In a nutshell, *hesed* is the gospel lived out.[5]

Our persistent search for love as humans is a search for what we had in perfection before the fall. *Hesed* is not something we were only designed to receive from God but what we're also supposed to give to one another. It is in this environment of faithful giving and receiving that we find true belonging. Here our hearts are satisfied in God and one another as we are known deeply and know others in the same way.

Habit of Resistance | Service

As great as all of this giving and receiving sounds, our "love blind spot" makes this difficult to put into practice. Committed and faithful love requires that, in our human relationships, we seek first to give, not to receive. Though a cliche, this small perspective shift is powerful. But since the emotional pull of our hearts is almost irresistible, and the way we've been formed by our culture is so well-established by past habits, we need a strong counter-habit to help us resist. We need something that will create within us a muscle memory for *hesed* love—something that helps us experience the love we desire and were created to have even when our hearts can't see clearly. That habit is *service.*

Learning from Jesus

In the Gospels, Jesus is asked more than 300 questions and only answers a few of them directly. Often, he answers with questions of his own to stir up thoughtful reflection in the minds of his listeners. Other times, he responds by telling a story and then asking a follow-up question.

In Luke 10, Jesus uses this multi-layered approach when someone asks him a question about what is needed to inherit eternal life. Jesus answers by asking the man what is written in the Law. The man responds by saying, "Love the Lord your God with all your heart, with all your soul, with all your strength, and with all your mind," and "your neighbor as yourself" (v. 27). At this point, it seems like the man's question has been answered because Jesus tells him, "You've answered correctly. . . . Do this and you will live" (v. 28). But "wanting to justify himself," the man asks one more follow-up question to get clarity: "And who is my neighbor?" (v. 29). Graciously, Jesus responds by telling a now-famous story: the Good Samaritan.

In case you aren't familiar with this parable, it tells the story of a Jewish man who is beaten up, robbed, and left lying on the side of the road. Two Jewish religious figures (a priest and a Levite) see the man on the side of the road, but they pass him by. The hero of the story—the Samaritan man—takes the wounded man to an inn and pays for the innkeeper to care for him. After sharing this story, Jesus asks the man he's talking to, "Which of these three do you think proved to be a neighbor to the man who fell into the hands of the robbers?" (v. 36). The man's response proves to be the answer to the question he asked Jesus.

Jesus knew there was a question behind the question when the man asked him, "Who is my neighbor?" His request for a neighbor qualification was to justify his own inclinations for neighbor boundaries. He wanted confirmation from Jesus that his love only needed to go to a certain group of people that excluded the ones he thought undeserving of his love. This may have been why Jesus chose to answer his question with a story where a Samaritan saves a Jewish man. Since the Samaritans were looked down on by Jews, it would have been a shock to hear that two Jewish men passed by the wounded Jew, but a Samaritan—an enemy of the Jews and the least likely person to help—saved his life.

What is fascinating about this story is that the Samaritan doesn't just help the man get back on his feet and leave him to find his way home. Instead, he puts him on his own donkey and uses his own money to pay for this man's care, money he probably won't get back (vv. 34–35). The Good Samaritan didn't just serve this wounded Jewish man, he served him sacrificially. *This* is the type of behavior that Jesus equates with the call to love your neighbor as yourself. In the kingdom of God, this is what it means for us to love one another well.

In the end, Jesus not only told piercing stories of this kind of love—he displayed it himself on the cross, dying for his enemies. He didn't merely give up his own resources—he gave up his life. He is the living embodiment and display of God's *hesed*, and his demonstration of love is something we not only receive for ourselves in the gospel, it's something we imitate in our love for those around us.

A Selfless Love

Self-sacrificial service is a habit that helps us remember what biblical love requires and can produce. With each selfless act, we are trained to be people who put aside our personal desires to support the needs of others. These acts of service can be as small as cooking a meal for someone or as big as walking with them through a season of despair and darkness. Slowly over time, our consistent posture of humility and selflessness cultivates a space of belonging in our friendships, marriages, and any other close relationship we might have.

Think about it—when someone is trying to serve you, they usually aren't lying, withholding affection, shaming you, or doing any of the other things that make relationships sour. Instead, in wisdom, they are taking the initiative to go out of their way to better your life, even when that requires them to change, adjust, or heal emotionally. They are also willing to have hard accountability conversations because their driving goal is your good and God's glory.

I want you to pause for a few moments to imagine what your relationships would be like if this was how the other person showed up. Then, imagine what they would be like if you showed up this way. How would the relationship change? What would it include and what would it no longer have?

When I consider this, I picture relationships with less disappointment or hurt from unmet expectations. I could show up at any time in my brokenness without any fear that I'd be rejected or ridiculed. I'd have someone who was intentional about considering my well-being, and showing up accordingly. Even though it wouldn't be perfect, I think this person would feel a little like home.

While it's counterintuitive, this type of love can't be found simply by looking for the person who fits our list of preferences. It is true that there are some obvious traits that show us whether or not someone is capable of being in a healthy relationship, but biblical love is cultivated over time. In fact, I don't think we find it, but rather find someone we want to build it with.

Live It Out

Our culture's false story sounds like this: "Follow your heart to get love." But God's gospel story flies in its face: "No—receive the committed, sacrificial love only God can give in the person of Christ, and then instead of following your heart, follow God's love pattern. Then and only then will you know what real love is." When our hearts can't see well, the spiritual habit of service helps us do this. It helps us reconnect with a love we were created to have. Even though it might not produce the same immediate dopamine hit as infatuation, it forms a deeply rooted love that will be around long after those initial feelings of infatuation are gone.

To apply what you've just learned, this week ask the Holy Spirit to bring someone to mind that you can serve self-sacrificially. It might be someone you know, like your roommate, a family member, or close friend. It might be someone you aren't as familiar with, like a neighbor, coworker, or someone you regularly see at church but don't know well.

Then schedule a time to love them self-sacrificially by bringing them a meal, helping them with a chore/task, or sending them money to cover an expense they are burdened by. Or, on the other hand, the act of service could also be something more personal, like apologizing for a hurtful statement you made or the commitment you flaked on. As you are brainstorming your act of service, mark a time on your calendar to choose someone new to serve each month, because *our actions only become habits when we do them repeatedly!*

Friend, love, in all its beauty, was created by and is rooted in God. When we remember this, our love is beautiful and life-giving. When we forget, it becomes shallow and destructive. Our culture's story of selfishness leads us to forget. The Bible's story of selflessness helps us remember.

Now, I wouldn't be honest if I didn't mention that selflessness doesn't always produce long-lasting love. You can be as selfless as you want and still have an unhealthy relationship because the other person is not willing to show up in kind. Or, because we are prone to sin, in our attempts to be selfless we will inevitably hurt one another.

So what do we do when this happens? Great question. Let's answer it together in the next chapter.

Chapter 4

A Better Justice

"I had a friend-breakup today."

These are the words my friend Simone texted me a few months ago when I asked her how her day had been. She was emotionally overwhelmed, because a good friendship had suddenly soured, reaching the point of no return. The following day, I made my way to Simone's house. I arrived with good food and snacks in tow to help her process what had happened. As we sat around her dinner table she began to tell me what happened. Like many relationships, the pain points had started to develop slowly over time.

A dry spot in the relationship with fewer check-ins and one or two unanswered phone calls was deemed malicious rather than the overflow of a busy life season. Instead of addressing her concerns, Simone's former friend chose the passive-aggressive route. Indirect communication turned into arguments that then turned into a long text message from Simone's friend that described all the feelings she had been holding in and her choice to end the friendship.

By the time Simone finished telling this part of the story, we had finished dinner and were eating dessert. After hearing her describe a series of twists and turns, I responded by sharing my disappointment that something so small had resulted in the dissolution of a friendship. Even though Simone's friend had some bad relationship habits, she genuinely felt wronged by Simone's behavior. Cutting things off was her way of righting those wrongs and enacting justice. In her mind, an excommunication sentence was the appropriate judgment for my friend's social crime.

Justice is something we might not always have the words to describe, but it's something we can feel in our gut. In a moment, an internal alarm starts to go off, signaling that we have been wronged by someone. For some of us, it starts in our stomachs and makes its way to our faces, with furrowed eyebrows and squinted eyes expressing our disdain for the behavior that is negatively impacting us. For others, the alarm is directly connected to our mouths. We immediately start to share strong words that tell the guilty party they messed with the wrong person!

All of us are born with an internal justice alarm. Even babies have it. If you don't believe me, try snatching a toy away from a toddler and see what happens! Even though our sense of justice can be manipulated by people who confuse us about how we ought to be treated, most of us are born with the ability to know when someone's behavior moved into the "inappropriate and unacceptable zone."

When someone crosses the line, we feel like they have taken something from us and their theft has incurred a debt.

For our alarm to stop, they need to pay back what they owe us. Their payment, depending on the level of severity, could be anything from an apology to a prison sentence. Either way, our innate sense of justice requires that the wrong be righted before we can move on. We can't let it go, and maybe that's because in the beginning, God didn't let it go either.

Back to the Beginning

We've already talked about the curses God gives Adam and Eve, but I want us to revisit them. This time, let's consider God's choice to respond to their actions in this manner.

After Adam and Eve eat the fruit of the forbidden tree, God shows up. In Genesis 3:8, we are told that Adam and Eve hear God walking in the garden and they hide. It's as if they not only know their actions are wrong, but they don't want to face the One they disobeyed. Even though he knows where they are, God doesn't uncover their hiding spot. Instead, he calls out to them, asking where they are. What begins to transpire is a conversation where God asks Adam questions, even though he already knows the answers. With a subtle grace, God invites Adam to confess his wrongdoing. Adam responds by shifting blame to Eve—a cowardly way of admitting the wrongdoing.

This moment in history is the beginning of God's human experiment. With great intentionality and care, he has created a perfect world and allowed Adam and Eve to inhabit it. Furthermore, he graces them with his presence. Rather than creating the world and leaving for another project, God stayed to dwell with his creation. Adam and Eve were blessed with a perfect world and an unhindered, intimate, relationship with its Creator. Even with all this beauty given to them, Adam and Eve broke their relationship with God, violating the trust bond they once perfectly enjoyed with him.

How did God respond to this injustice done to him? God could have immediately wiped Adam and Eve off the face of the earth, abruptly ending his human experiment. He could have started over with two new humans, hoping that if faced with the same temptation they would make a different choice. Rather than replacing them or abandoning the relationship entirely, God mercifully chose to let them learn through consequences. As long as Adam and Eve lived, they would remember the way they had wronged God. However, Adam and Eve were not capable of repaying the debt that justice required. So within this list of curses is a promise that points to a greater truth—God will eventually pay their debt for them.

We see this promise in Genesis 3:15, where God says to Adam, Eve, and the serpent, "I will put hostility between you and the woman, and between your offspring and her offspring. He will strike your head, and you will strike his heel." The offspring of the woman is Christ and he will strike a fatal blow to the head of the enemy. Instead of leaving Adam and Eve to fend for themselves, God steps in and sends Christ to settle their debts for them.

As the sons and daughters of Adam and Eve, we inherited the same curses and the same sin-nature that they experienced, and like them, in big and small ways, we often violate the trust bond we have with God and others. Yet, through God's mercy (as we'll observe later in this chapter), our debt will also be paid. Given that God pays our debt to himself, you'd think that would make us tender toward those who wrong us. But when others wrong us and it's our turn to dish out justice, we are often tempted to do what God did not. Especially in our interpersonal relationships, we are quick to judge and slow to extend mercy.

Our Culture's Story: *Merciless Vengeance*

Anyone who knows me knows I love documentaries. Most years, I watch more documentaries than any other type of film. Recently, I watched one about a popular music artist. The movie documented her rise to fame and the highs and lows of her journey. It included footage from the very beginning of her career, with the artist singing at football games and family cookouts. It was evident that her commitment to her music helped her beat the odds and gain traction, both in the U.S. and overseas. But in the middle of her success, she hit a low point when a controversy almost led to her getting canceled.

As you likely already know, "canceled" is when the general public corporately decides that your actions are unredeemable. Critics use our favorite communication tool, social media, to express their distrust and dislike with messages that range from death threats to body-shaming, name-calling, and a downright meanness that would bring the strongest person to tears. Many people have had "trolls" or "haters" comment on their posts, but when someone is being canceled, the number of people making these comments is massive—sometimes in the thousands or even millions. Eventually the momentum grows to be so much that a person's character is tarnished, leaving them unable to show their face for a long time, if at all.

The music artist whose documentary I watched got into a dispute with another public figure that eventually resulted in them pressing criminal charges against the artist. While the evidence showed that this musician had been the victim of a crime, the public thought differently. The movie showed clip after clip of those far from her story and the situation—podcasters, YouTubers, and social media folks—commenting about how she was lying. Those with little access to the facts seemed to have the biggest (and loudest) opinions.

I'll be honest—it was hard to watch all the commentary, most of which was really gossip. Alongside the clips about criticism and hate, the film showed how this musician's mental and emotional health deteriorated quickly. People were so confidently critical about an event they did not have firsthand knowledge of. They had become judge and jury, deciding that based on the evidence of their personal opinions, this artist no longer deserved her dignity or career. The "wrong" this artist had committed required her to be wiped off the face of the earth. Redemption was not possible.

What made this element of the documentary so moving was that it pointed to a pattern of behavior that is common online. Every so often, a scandal comes to light, and we all become amateur FBI agents trying to figure out what happened. As people put the details together on their own, they start forming opinions about the story. These opinions then become fact as we decide the person in question is guilty before they are proven innocent.

Whether the offense is real or perceived, we respond like we have been wronged and air out our grievances on the internet. Instead of pausing to leave space for nuance, complexity, or mercy, we decide there is only one way to resolve the situation. To repay their debt to society, the offender must cease to exist.

What is worse is that our "public justice" tactics are showing up offline, as we use these same tools to navigate issues of interpersonal conflict.

Formed by Culture

Here is the uncomfortable truth: We love vengeance. We love watching someone suffer negative consequences when they have done us or someone else wrong. As mentioned earlier, when we experience injustice, the person who has treated us wrongly incurs a debt that isn't satisfied until we feel like the debt is paid in full. But most of the time, we never get that feeling because we like the feeling of them owing us more than we do the feeling of setting them free.

Cancel culture fuels our love for vengeance. It helps us bypass the uncomfortable and inconvenient phase of forgiveness and reconciliation. Instead of processing our grievances with someone directly, we learn to lean on indirect communication like DMs and text messages. Furthermore, we process the situation in an echo chamber full of people who won't challenge our views but instead support us wholeheartedly.

Now, please hear me out—I am not dismissing some of the horrible things many of us have experienced. Some people commit wrong acts against us with no remorse. They don't care if we forgive them and might do the same thing to us again. These situations require wisdom, as certain boundaries might need to be put in place so you can forgive them from a distance as reconciliation might not be safe or possible.

Some injustices are so reprehensible they deserve nothing less than a long prison sentence. Other wrongdoings have been perpetrated by large groups of people and governments, like racism, genocide, and human trafficking. Again, in these situations we are not supposed to just accept an apology and move on. As with personal relationships, the damage caused is deep, and reconciliation requires boundaries and guidelines for systemic change.

However, since many wonderful books have been written on these justice issues, they are not the focus of this chapter. Rather, I want us to focus on the way we are being shaped to handle injustices in our personal relationships, with our family, friends, and neighbors. It might be someone who disrespected you with their words, a coworker who is maligning your character, a friend who betrayed your confidence by lying to you, or a neighbor flying a flag that supports a political candidate you strongly oppose.

In these relationships, cancel culture is training us to be people who are slow to listen, quick to speak, and quick to anger. Relationship dynamics are often layered and complicated, which means the path to resolution requires us to sit in the tension longer than we'd like. It also requires us to rehumanize the person who has wronged us, but when we do this, it becomes difficult to take vengeance against them. In our desire for quick, uncomplicated results, we make rash and unwise conflict mediation decisions.

We've also been trained to prioritize passive-aggressive conflict resolution techniques. Instead of taking our anger to the Lord, we first head online. We would prefer making videos to show our frustration rather than expressing it directly to the person. Or we take it to our community, telling everyone but the person involved what has happened. Our desire for support becomes a breeding ground for gossip as we search for people who will let us talk without challenging our views.

The more we prioritize vengeance, we eventually grow more and more comfortable with unforgiveness. We normalize making it impossible for someone to pay off the debt their offense incurred. In part, this is because we enjoy the power we get to have over other people when we are arbiters of justice. Whether it's through a petty response or social ostracism (e.g., cutting someone off), we justify our unforgiveness because we've come to believe wrongdoers don't deserve mercy.

But that's until we are in a situation where *we need it.*

God's Story: *Merciful Justice*

Second Samuel 24 is an odd passage. It is the last chapter in the two-part story of the beginning of Israel's monarchy. First and 2 Samuel detail Israel's request for a king, and the reign of their first two kings, Saul and David. Chapter 24 comes at the end of David's reign. At first glance, it seems to be a bit out of place, as the previous chapter includes David's last words. But, like I've said before, I've learned that when something looks like it doesn't belong, it's an invitation for me to read slowly, as there is probably a message within the passage that is easily missed.

This chapter tells the story of a situation in which David took a census, counting the number of fighting men in Israel and Judah. Taking a census was common practice, and we even have record of God ordering Israel to do so several times in the book of Numbers (Num. 1:2; 4:2, 22; 26:2). However, this census was deemed to be sinful as David himself confesses that he should not have taken it. While it is not explicitly given in the text, scholars believe it was because David was fueling his pride by seeing the large size of his army.[1] Feeling the guilt of his wrongdoing, David asks the Lord for a path of redemption to make right his sinful action. The Lord obliges and lets David choose his punishment from one of three options: three years of famine, three months fleeing from his enemies, or three days of a plague in the land.

Remember how I said there was a message that could be easily missed in this odd chapter? Well, we find it in David's response to God's multiple-choice punishment list. He says, "Please, let us fall into the LORD's hands because his mercies are great, but don't let me fall into human hands" (2 Sam. 24:14). When given a chance to choose between judgment from God and judgment from others, David chooses God. His reason is startling: God had more mercy than humans.

David made a decision based upon the truth of God's character he knew intimately. Even when David sins against

Bathsheba, Uriah, and ultimately God, God does not kill David.[2] Instead, He mercifully spares his life. Through confession and repentance, he allows David back into fellowship with him. David writes about this in Psalm 51, saying, "Have mercy on me, O God, according to your unfailing love; according to your great compassion blot out my transgressions" (Ps. 51:1 NIV). It was God's love, his *hesed*, that fueled his mercy and compassion. As a man who had been deeply impacted by the mercy of God, when given the opportunity to be helped by it, David does not hesitate to say yes.

In his mercy, God still allows David to experience the consequences of his actions. From the options given by God, David chooses option #3, the plague. For three days, God rains down judgment on Israel. While it is harsh, it is limited, and after three days, the plague ends. In addition to God's mercy, in this passage we see a demonstration of his justice. It's as if the two are intertwined, working at the same time in God's response to David's sin. While God is fair in his judgment of David, not over- or under-punishing him, he is also merciful, because he didn't give David the full extent of what he deserved.

This dynamic points to God's unity, the reality that all his attributes are at work in his whole being at all times. They are never in opposition. Since God is eternal and unchanging, his justice has always been both fair and merciful at the same time.

Formed by God

I wish I could say that I have always been a diligent worker, but I haven't. So much so that my lack of diligence almost got me fired. In one of my first jobs, I had a difficult time staying at my desk. I worked in an isolated area in the office, so people didn't come by my desk often. A guy I liked worked in another department and every so often I'd go by his office and spend a little too much time there. A few weeks of this behavior turned into a few months, and my work performance started to slip. To make up for it, I started to cut corners and miss steps that my work projects required.

Eventually my sloppiness led to a big mistake that could have cost my company a significant amount of money. When I realized my mistake, and that there was no way for me to remedy it on my own, I had to tell my boss. Looking back, she should have fired me on the spot. But, after giving me a long and hard "get it together or we WILL fire you" pep talk, my boss put me on a performance plan to help me get back on track.

I walked back to my desk, sat in my chair, and just stared at my computer screen. I felt deeply embarrassed—not just because of the mistake itself, but because my boss had to give me such a hard wake-up call. But I was also shocked that I still had my job. The night before, I had run scenarios in my head about how the meeting with my boss would go. Only a few of them ended with me not walking out the door with a box full of my personal belongings. Even though I deserved a harsher punishment, my boss chose to show me mercy.

The following day, I showed up to work with a new resolve. Since I had been the recipient of compassion, I wanted my work to reflect my gratitude. Additionally, this moment would also affect me in future years when I was leading my own staff team. It made me more gracious, understanding, and willing to give people a second chance. The mercy I had received from my boss made me a more merciful boss. I chose to share what I had been given.

Through Christ, you and I are the recipients of God's mercy. Instead of experiencing the full extent of the consequences of our sin, through Christ our debt has been paid in full. When I think about this, one phrase usually pops into my mind: *God didn't have to, but he did.* God was under no obligation to show us mercy. He had no reason to withhold from us the eternal death that should have been ours because of our sin. But because of his mercy, we have an eternity in paradise with him to look forward to.

When we allow it, this mercy also has the power to transform us in the here and now. It should make us people who are more patient, less prone to be offended, and more willing to forgive. Rather than revel in acts of vengeance, we find joy in honoring God's gift to us by releasing others from the debts their offenses have accumulated.

Habit of Resistance | Confession and Forgiveness

Our culture's false story of merciless vengeance encourages us to allow our love for payback to drive our handling of offense, leading us to hand out punishments that have no end date. But God's story encourages us to handle situations of offense in light of the mercy we have received from him. But since the sting of offense and the pull of vengeance is so strong, we need strong habits to develop our ability to show mercy. Those habits are *confession* and *forgiveness*.

Learning from Jesus

This makes me think of the parable Jesus taught about an unforgiving servant in Matthew 18:21–35. It's a story that Jesus tells in response to a question Peter asks concerning how many times he needed to forgive someone who sins against him. Thinking he was being generous, Peter offered seven as a possible option. To his surprise, Jesus responds by recommending that Peter should forgive seventy times seven, or 490 times. He then shares the story about the unforgiving servant.

The story begins by introducing a king who uncovered a large debt from one of his servants, who we'll call "the man." The king brings this man before him and orders that he and his whole family be sold into slavery to pay the debt—a debt which amounted to about twenty years' wages for a laborer.[3] But the man begged for mercy, asking for patience and assuring the king that if he gave him time, he'd pay back everything. Hearing this, the king was moved with compassion and forgave the man's entire debt.

The man then left and found a fellow servant who owed him money. He grabbed him, started choking him, and said, "'Pay what you owe!'" (Matt. 18:28). The servant begged for mercy, but the man refused to give it to him and threw him into prison until he could pay back his debt—a debt which amounted to about one day's wage.[4] The folks who were watching and who knew the man's debts had been forgiven went and told the king what had happened. Needless to say, the king was furious at the man for having just been forgiven a *twenty-year* debt, only to turn around and hold his friend's feet to the fire for a *one-day* debt. The king reprimanded the man for his lack of compassion and threw him in jail where he would be tortured until he could pay back his debts.

The story ends with Jesus saying: "So also my heavenly Father will do to you unless every one of you forgives his brother or sister from your heart" (v. 35).

Needless to say, Jesus's multilayered answer is meant to evoke a strong response. On one hand, we can relate to the reaction of the man who, despite having his debt forgiven, still tried to collect what he was owed. We know the sharp sting of offense. While reading his story, we might think about someone who has incurred a debt against us. As we walk through that memory, the anger starts to rise in our spirit as we think about how to regain what was stolen from us, whether it was our dignity, reputation, or time.

On the other hand, the man had just been forgiven of a large debt. It's shocking how quickly he forgot, how his attitude switched from gratitude to vengeance as he refused to offer the servant the same patience and compassion the king had offered him. Even after the servant begged him for mercy. And, then if this wasn't enough, Jesus provides a sharp warning at the end.

In this story, we are the man. We tend to forget the gift of mercy and compassion we have received from God. The debt of sin we owe God is insurmountable. We couldn't pay it even if we tried. How appalling would it be for us to experience God's forgiveness for a *lifetime*'s worth of our own sin, and yet be unwilling to forgive a *moment*'s worth of sin when someone wrongs us? How absurd would it be for us to be forgiven by God for offending him on the *cosmic* level of treason, only to turn around and hold one of our peers hostage for minor, *earthly* offenses? The truth is that we don't have to imagine doing such a thing; we do this every day. Like the man, it is easy for us to forget how many times we've offended God, and how much we've been forgiven. Especially as we are sitting in the moment of being personally offended by a friend and maybe even dealing with shame and ridicule from the people who are watching us.

Here's the thing—sharing mercy doesn't make you popular, may not help you get ahead relationally, and sometimes, like the king, it will cost you because you have to absorb the debt. However, we don't do it for our own benefit. We do it to bring glory to God. We share mercy to model to the world a better way of handling conflict, showing people the way of the kingdom. The hope is that in the same way that God's mercy has transformed us, others will be transformed when we share mercy with them.

Now, you might read this and think I'm providing a naive or oversimplified response to our culture's way of dealing with wrongdoers. You might be saying, *"I don't know about this, Elizabeth. This feels like a sugary Christian response."*

I get it. The idea of showing mercy can seem impractical or even foolish. It can make us feel like we are letting people off the hook or empowering them to repeat the same offense with someone else. But remember—God's mercy doesn't cancel out his justice. It simply means the judgment he gives his children has limits. Hebrews 12:6 tells us that God is in the habit of letting his children experience the consequences of their behavior. He does this as a deterrent for future sin and to encourage people to walk on the path of holiness.

However, God is also perfectly just; he alone knows the appropriate judgment for any offense and is the only one perfectly qualified to enact it. This is why he tells us to leave the vengeance to him (Rom. 12:19). Any act of sin is ultimately an offense to God, so whether it's through Christ on the cross, through the final judgment of Revelation 20, or somewhere in between, God will take care of every offense in the perfect manner it needs to be taken care of.

So the offenses people commit against us should not be without consequence. And sometimes the consequence needs to be harsh. But we shouldn't be people who are driven by our love for vengeance. We shouldn't normalize the belief that people are unredeemable. Our justice should have limits because the One who is perfectly just limits how he judges us. Instead of responding with unforgiveness, pettiness, social ostracization, retaliation, gossip, or passive-aggressiveness, our responsibility as God's children is to share the merciful justice that has been shared with us.

Walking Back Toward Mercy

Similar to the way the habit of prayer helps us resist false versions of peace and pursue true peace (seen in chapter 2), resisting our culture's justice tactics and pursuing merciful justice is one that also begins in prayer. But this time, a specific *kind* of prayer time is what I want to emphasize.

Often pride and self-righteousness prevent us from handling conflict with humility. Pride quietly convinces us that we are better than someone else, making it hard for us to see and own our shortcomings. It can also lead us to justify our behavior based upon what someone else did to us. For all these reasons and more, we need the practice of coming before God—who can see the full story and knows the right way of handling it—with total honesty. It is here that the Holy Spirit can place us in a posture of humility so that we are more apt to share the mercy that has been given to us.

This time of prayer, if we use it well, becomes a time of *confession* and *forgiveness.* It is an opportunity for us to not only ask the Lord to reveal the pride in our hearts, but also to ask him to show us the places that we are harboring unforgiveness, bitterness, and fear. There are some prayers I believe the Holy Spirit answers on the spot, and this is one of them. When he reveals to us the places that need to be reclaimed by his mercy, we can confess our sin and repent.

Sometimes, in prayer, God reveals to us that our confession needs to also be made to the person we have wronged. While this takes a lot of courage and humility, the practice of confession reminds us that we are sinners in need of forgiveness and grace from God.

The act of confession helps us train the muscles that empower us to forgive, because no one gives mercy better than the person who is deeply persuaded that he needs it himself and is being given it in Christ.[5] Unforgiveness is a form of self-protection. We often think that by withholding forgiveness from people, we are protecting ourselves from future hurt. In reality, unforgiveness chains us to the past and prevents true healing and reconciliation. While the restoration of the relationship may not be possible, we are still able to extend the mercy that we received from God by blessing and forgiving those who have wounded us, releasing them from the relational debt they have incurred.

Live It Out

Our culture's false story sounds like this: "Wrongdoers don't deserve second chances—show no mercy and make them pay back everything they owe you." But God's gospel story is radically different: "No—remember the mercy God showed you for your sins. Then share that same mercy to others. This might include consequences, but choose them in light of God's mercy, not your desire for vengeance."

When the sting of offense tempts us to forget God's story and walk in the way of the world, the habits of confession and forgiveness give us the gospel jolt we need to push back against conventional wisdom and walk in the way of Christ. It helps us remember our responsibility to share the overflow of mercy we have received. While this means we will often forfeit the immediate gratification of vengeance, we exchange it for something much greater—an opportunity to cultivate shalom and glorify God.

To help you lean into what you've just learned, choose one day this week to spend an extended time practicing the habit of confession in prayer. Take a few moments to reflect on the past few days or weeks, asking the Holy Spirit to reveal to you any sin that you have committed against God and others (i.e., family, friends, coworkers). Walk through each sin with God, asking for his forgiveness. As you do this, remember that our God is compassionate, gentle, and loving. His mercy welcomes us as we confess our sin, and he does not condemn us (Rom. 8:1; 1 John 1:9).

During your time of confession, ask the Holy Spirit to bring to mind anyone you might have sinned against. Confess your sin to God and then spend time thinking of how you can help mend the situation or relationship. You could call them to make an apology, or set up a time for you to ask for their forgiveness in person. Don't let the fear of embarrassment or rejection hold you back. Even if the situation doesn't go perfectly, do your best to honor God as you talk with them.

Repeat this practice at least once a week, setting aside intentional time to consider your own sin and asking God and others for forgiveness. As you are regularly reminded of your need for mercy and God's willingness to share it with you, pay attention to how this impacts your response when other people sin against or offend you. Hopefully, what you notice is that in addition to an increase in patience and understanding, you are more prone to share with them the same mercy you regularly receive from God.

Chapter 5

A Better Joy

Have you ever said to yourself or to someone else, "I just want to be happy"?

I have.

Just a few weeks ago, I was talking with a friend, expressing my frustration about a difficult situation I was navigating. She asked me what I wanted, and after pausing to think about my answer, I responded with that six-word phrase.

In our contemporary evangelical culture, the word *happiness* has gotten a bad reputation. We often pit it against joy, presenting happiness as less valuable because it's based upon our circumstances, while joy is a permanent disposition that comes from our relationship with God. One pastor described this distinction by saying, "Happiness is a light-hearted, worldly feeling, but joy is a God-feeling."

I don't necessarily agree with this, though, because I rarely hear people say, "I just want to be more joyful." What we desire in life isn't complex enough for us to create a substantive distinction between joy and happiness. I think for many of us, the two are intertwined. We use the words interchangeably because they point us to the same thing—good feelings of fulfillment and satisfaction that last over time.

To minimize confusion, I will be using the word joy for the rest of the chapter.

Our experience of joy can come from many different places. Sometimes, we find joy in nature. While most of my interaction with nature is from the inside of a building that has a great view of the outdoors, even I know that a butterfly, rainbow, or fresh snowfall can lift our spirits and bring light to our eyes.

For others, joy comes from art or music. Maybe for you it comes from the accomplishment of finishing a work project, or the endorphins you get after a HIIT workout session. Or, if you are like me, joy comes from eating a good meal with great friends! Much of our lived experiences produce these "good feelings." Since joy is both powerful and intoxicating, it is natural that we would not want our experience of it to end.

Unfortunately, our desire for joy can also arise out of challenging situations. Suffering, longing, disappointment, and fear can suffocate our hearts, taking up any room that joy might have previously occupied. As I reflect on my own seasons of loss and heartbreak, my grief made it feel like joy had taken an indefinite vacation. In these vulnerable moments, I longed for anything to take away the pain and fill my heart with joy.

A desire for joy is universal and, like the other characteristics we will discuss in this book, our pursuit of it is not problematic or unbiblical. Instead, it hearkens back to the first few moments of creation, where joy makes its first appearance in the world.

Back to the Beginning

Repetition is one of my favorite teaching tools. I love repetition because when it's done well, it's a simple but effective way to help people remember the most important parts of my message. I think most people struggle to remember what they hear or read. So, even though I like to vary my teaching style, repetition is one tool I always use.

I'm obviously not the first person to use repetition in this manner. In speaking and writing, it's been used by a lot of people for a long time. We even see repetition in the Bible, especially in the first chapter of the first book. This first account of the creation of the world uses repetition both poetically and practically, making the passage beautiful and bringing attention to specific details in the story.

Of the many examples we could pull from, for this chapter, we'll focus on one word that's repeated seven times in Genesis 1—"good" (Gen. 1:4, 10, 12, 18, 21, 25, 31). After speaking each part of creation into existence, the author of Genesis tells us, "God saw that it was **good** (emphasis mine)." This word *good* is the English translation of the Hebrew word *tov*. Throughout the creation narrative, *tov* is used to communicate God's artistry in all that he creates. Every time God declares creation good, he is celebrating its beauty and excellence while simultaneously showing how it is pleasing and delightful.[1] This celebration builds with each mention of *tov* and it climaxes in verse 31, when God declares that all he has created is very good or *tov me'od.* It's as if he throws his hands up in the air and yells out, "Very well done! Perfect! What a masterpiece!"[2]

These moments of celebration are the first glimpse of joy we see in Scripture. What is interesting is that the person we see embodying joy is not Adam or Eve but God. His celebration is so grand, that on the seventh day God rests to celebrate and reflect some more. The writer of Psalm 104:31 highlights this when he says, "May the glory of the LORD endure forever; may the LORD rejoice in his works." The word *rejoice* directly relates to God's work of creating the world!

Graciously, God doesn't keep all the joy to himself. He created humanity for many reasons, but one was to share his joy by living in paradise alongside him. If creation was so good that God had to celebrate it, then imagine what effect it would have on us!

As Creator, God finds joy in what he has brought into existence, and since he is the One that brought it to life, ultimately he is finding joy in himself. This means he is the Source and Origin of our joy, not his creation—a vital distinction that makes all the difference. For this reason, our divinely inspired pursuit of joy becomes problematic when we get confused about *where* joy comes from.

Our Culture's Story: *The Joy of Overconsumption*

Extreme Home Makeover was a reality TV show from the early 2000s that helped families remodel their entire home.

Most of the families featured on the show had some type of need. Their home might have been affected by a hurricane or severe fire damage. Sometimes the need was a physical ailment; a family member might have been disabled or injured in a car crash. Sadly, some stories were about families who had tragically lost a child or parent. Every episode contained some type of hardship that brought tears to your eyes.

The premise of the show was simple—the renovation team would show up to surprise the family, kick them out of their house for a week, renovate the house, and then reveal the renovations to the family. At the reveal, the house would be blocked by a bus. The show host, Ty Pennington, would then shout his famous line "Move . . . that . . . bus!"

The reveal was paired with a house tour, so the family and millions of viewers could see all the upgrades that had been made to the home. Sometimes the renovations included home additions, where the size of the house had been significantly increased. This seemed like the perfect blessing for families who were in need. But, for some, it ended up being the opposite.

After the TV crew and renovation team left, many families began to experience hardship that was tied to their renovated homes. While for some this meant repeated break-ins, the biggest burden was the increase in home bills. For some homeowners, electric bills grew to amounts exceeding their pre-renovation mortgages simply to cover the cost of all their new electronic gadgets and appliances. Others were faced with property taxes they could not afford.

Unfortunately, some of these families ended up selling or foreclosing on their homes because the cost of the home expansion was too much for them to bear.

When I think back to these *Extreme Home Makeover* episodes, the TV show's prescribed solution to the problems these families were facing was to give them more. The more came in the form of increased quantity and quality. They were given bigger houses, more electronics, and new furniture and appliances. The hope was that their woes would be soothed and joy increased by a new and improved home. While some of them genuinely needed some upgrades and help getting out of a desperate situation, the point remains that most of these cases didn't account for the fact that their newfound, temporary abundance could only provide a limited amount of joy.

While most of us aren't trying to find joy by getting our house renovated on TV, we are tempted by the same belief that our joy is directly connected to what we have. Through creative advertising, our culture continually invites us to believe that the solution for our joy problem is to consume more.

On TV, we continually see ads from companies like Apple or Disney that rarely share the cost of what they are selling. Rather, they present a visually appealing story about how your life will benefit from purchasing their product or experience. Whether the benefit is increased productivity or family memories, it is always presented as a pathway to increased joy.

On social media, these same stories are being given to us by our favorite influencers. Posts about shopping hauls, top Amazon finds, and home decor frequently include a link to a website where we can quickly purchase the item. I'll admit, these posts are enticing. It's hard to not be pulled in by a photo or video that has perfect lighting and editing. These posts are often personalized, as influencers invite us to follow them for a "day in the life" or a "get ready with me" video. For a moment, they seem just like us. As we watch their post we can think, *Maybe, if I have what they have, I'll have as much joy as they seem to have in this post.* And within a few seconds, we've clicked the product link, put it in our shopping cart, and hit "buy."

But while these posts seem organic, many of these influencers are paid by companies to promote their products. These business partnerships have had a massive economic impact, with influencer marketing estimated to become a $24 billion industry by the end of 2024.[3] Businesses are spending big money to get us to spend money.

Now, I'm not suggesting that these products aren't helpful or aren't worth investing in, because sometimes they are. However, we need to realize that our culture's invitation to consume ***never stops***. As long as we keep scrolling, we keep being inundated with posts that impact how we spend our money and steward our time.

When we believe that joy comes from doing what feels good, *we will do whatever feels good*. Hitting that "buy" button *feels good*, getting the Amazon package in the mail *feels good*, and wearing our new outfit or seeing a new piece of furniture in our home *feels good*. In fact, these things feel so good, we keep doing them. Whether it's a consumer good or something more illicit, if joy comes from consuming, then we will keep consuming without limitation because we need another joy boost.

Formed by Culture

However, our pursuit of unlimited consumption is not without consequences. It is forming us, both individually and corporately. On one hand, our consumption habits are affecting the environment. Whether it's the rising heat in Europe, long-term drought in Northwestern Africa, or the severe tropical storms in India and Bangladesh, our world is experiencing an increase in extreme weather and climate events. Scientists point to a significant increase in greenhouse gasses like carbon dioxide as one of the causes for these climate changes.[4] While this increase can be linked to many factors, a prominent one is overconsumption.

In addition to climate change, our purchasing habits are impacting the people who create the items we buy. With many major corporations producing their items overseas, it has been more common to hear news stories about the working conditions in many of these factories. One of our motivators to buy more is because of low prices, which sometimes are related to unjust business practices. Many corporations pay their workers poorly and do not invest in safe working conditions. These lower costs keep profit margins high, as these companies continue to meet our ever-increasing consumption demands.

On the other hand, our habits are affecting us personally. While overconsumption brings us momentary joy, it leaves behind long-term impact. For example, many of our homes are filled with products we don't use. This has become more evident with the growth of the decluttering trend. After watching shows like *Tidying Up with Marie Kondo* or *Get Organized with the Home Edit*, many of us ran to our closets or kitchens to throw out or donate the stuff we didn't need anymore. However, this doesn't mean we have stopped buying stuff. In fact, many of these decluttering influencers encourage us to buy their custom containers to organize the items we have left. And if this is news to you, just go to YouTube and type "decluttering" into the search bar to see how many people have documented their paring-down process for us.

Alongside homes that are overfilled, our rates of consumer debt keep growing. At the time of this writing, Americans owe about $1.21 trillion in credit card debt.[5] The truth about debt is that regardless of the reason it was acquired, it often places a burden on us, financially and mentally. How many of us are carrying these unnecessary burdens because we overspend? Or how many of us have a reduced ability to be generous with our money because of what we overspend?

Now, before you close the book because my observations and questions feel a little too piercing, I want you to pause, take a deep breath, and think about who our culture is forming us into when they invite us to find joy in getting more. Our acceptance of their invitation forms our heart, shaping what we love and prioritize. Slowly and subtly, this heart transformation is making us gluttonous and discontent. The more we pursue the next "joy opportunity," the less we notice what we already have. The more we consume, the more difficult it is for us to believe that what we have is enough to meet our needs, especially our need for joy.

Left unchecked, this false story will produce within us an insatiable appetite, as we look to creation to do what can only be done by our Creator. Sadly, this will lead us to exploit for our personal gain the creation we were created to steward for God's glory.

God's Story: *The Joy of Communion*

The David we read about in Scripture is a complicated person. His life contains so many praiseworthy moments while also being fraught with blameworthy ones. David spends years fighting for his life as he patiently waits to reach the throne God set him apart for. But, while ruling as king, his own sinful proclivities result in a slew of family tragedies that include rape, incest, and death.

Needless to say, David wrestled with a lot of pain. Thankfully, however, some of this wrestling has been recorded for us in the Psalms. Almost 50 percent of the Psalms were authored by David, and many of these include strong language. In many of these songs and prayers to God, David does not hold back in describing his situation. His words are honest and vulnerable. They provide a peek inside the mind of a man who had everything the world says we should desire. Yet his words show that the power, wealth, women, and prestige he acquired were not enough to bring him lasting joy. Especially, in his psalms of lament, David's words leave the reader with the impression that the created things he enjoyed during his kingly reign had lost their luster. He needed something or Someone greater to sustain him in times of difficulty.

This complicated dynamic makes an appearance in Psalm 16. David's opening words clearly communicate his trepidation, as his life circumstances have once again turned sour, "Protect me, God, for I take refuge in you" (v. 1).

David quickly shifts his reflection from his pain to God. He says, "I said to the Lord, 'You are my Lord; I have nothing good besides you.' . . . Lord, you are my portion and my cup of blessing; you hold my future. The boundary lines have fallen for me in pleasant places; indeed, I have a beautiful inheritance" (vv. 2, 5–6). Immediately after asking God for protection, David describes his view of God. In a moment where he feels danger closing in, he takes cover in God.

David's words make me think of a phrase my father used to say when I was growing up: "Don't just pay attention to what people say, pay attention to what they don't say." This wise saying is a reminder that when obvious things are left out of a conversation, they are usually worth noting. For example, if you cooked a meal for your friends, you might ask them how they think it tasted. If they respond with comments that are unrelated to the food's quality, like "It's interesting" or "It seems like you're trying out something new," they are leaving out a key piece of information. When people's comments about your food mention everything but the taste, it probably means your food is not tasty.

In these opening verses of Psalm 16, what David does not say or do is notable. He is experiencing a moment of vulnerability and does not turn to his possessions or power to remedy it. Instead, he turns to God.

David sees God as his Source from which the goodness in his life flows. He is the beneficiary of the overflow from a good God, and it is in this that he delights or finds joy. Specifically, David acknowledges how God's goodness includes limitations, but he simultaneously acknowledges that these limitations are good.

Definitions matter. So this is what I mean when I say that God is good: *God is what is best and gives what is best. He is incapable of doing harm.*[6] David believes that whatever God bestows upon him is what is best. We can see this in the words he uses to close this psalm, "You reveal the path of life to me; in your presence is abundant joy; at your right hand are eternal pleasures" (v. 11). God is David's source of joy. No matter the season or situation, David can experience joy because his joy is rooted in the Creator, rather than created things.

The issue with our pursuit of joy is not our *desire* for joy, but the places we start looking for it. When our starting place is creation, we will use people, possessions, and experiences to fill our cup. However, creation is limited; the delight it brings to our lives is beautiful, but lacking. For a variety of different reasons, it fades away, leaving us looking for another created thing to take its place.

Formed by God

If you have any connection to the '90s, you'll understand why one of my favorite things to do as a kid was look through the Sears catalog during the Christmas season. This catalog was big! It contained hundreds of pages full of toys, clothing items, home goods, and anything any adult or child could ever want for Christmas. I remember grabbing the catalog from our mail pile and flipping through the toy section. As I circled all the things I wanted for Christmas, I could feel myself getting happier. I was so excited about getting the things I had seen. In fact, as the weeks went by, my excitement grew more and more.

Then, on Christmas Day, I saw which of my circled requests I had received! My little heart was full of so much joy as I unwrapped my gifts. The joy continued over the next few days as I began to play with my new toys. But after a few weeks or maybe months, it started to wane. Instead of looking to my new toys for joy, I started looking for something else that could fill that spot for me.

Here's why I share that story—there is no amount of created things that can give you an ultimate, lasting experience of joy. Creation was never designed to function in this way. God is the only Giver of life. Only he is the Divine Source, the point of origin from which all life flows. He is also the One who maintains and sustains the divine masterpiece of the universe. Creation is not self-sustaining; all that it needs to exist continually comes from God.

Think about it—have you ever noticed that even in smog-filled cities, we have air that continues to fill our lungs. We also live on an earth that has never stopped rotating on its axis with a force of gravity that never ceases to keep our feet on the ground. While for many of us these things go unnoticed, if they stopped our lives would be dramatically impacted. This is only a small part of what our Divine Designer does to ensure his creation continues to experience the life he created them to have, even if it is life in a sin-infected world.

So if God is our sustainer, this means that our starting place for our pursuit of joy needs to be in him, not his limited creation. While we can find delight in creation, it is not strong enough to sustain our need for joy. We can see this dynamic right now in our world. Our overconsumption requires too much from nature. We are consuming natural resources quicker than the earth can replenish them. We are also producing toxins quicker than the atmosphere can purify them. Creation is beginning to crumble under the weight of our demands.

God, however, is strong enough to provide whatever we need indefinitely. Since he is limitless, he will never tire, lose power, break down, or malfunction. Furthermore, since he is the sustainer of life, he is already at work in our lives to provide what we need, including joy. In our waking hours and while we sleep, God is continually working to sustain us with an outpouring of his goodness, filling our lives with good gifts and blessings (James 1:17; Matt. 7:11).

Since we live in a culture that prides itself on self-sufficiency, we can be prone to forget how much of our lives is sustained by the goodness of God. Our overconfidence in our own abilities causes us to give credit to ourselves when we should be giving it to God. All we are and all we have is because of him. In the words of Luke, "For in him we live and move and have our being" (Acts 17:28).

When we internalize the truth that God sustains us, our perspective shifts, and suddenly we see that what we really desire we already have. Joy is no longer something that we need to chase. Instead, it is waiting to be recognized all around us and ultimately in God. God has surrounded us with tangible and intangible things that we can delight in. Part of this delight comes from the consumption of creation, like a good meal, concert, or a new pair of earrings. But this consumption is more celebratory than self-sustaining. We consume from a place of contentment, seeking to delight in things that point us to God. However, this type of consumption is limited. We don't need to keep filling up our cup because it already overflows from unlimited goodness that comes from our unlimited God.

This means that when we believe our lives truly lack joy, the issue isn't that God missed us on one of his joy distribution runs. Rather, we have drifted from the Source. We have given precious space in our hearts to created things that really belongs to the Creator. To find our way back home, we need something that will help us reclaim that space for God.

Habit of Resistance | Fasting

Our culture's false story tells us to find joy in what we can consume. Whether it's through material goods or experiences, we have become stuck in our habits of overconsumption trying to meet our need for joy. Like I mentioned earlier, in order to get "unstuck" or to push against this false story, we can't simply acknowledge it, we have to live differently. One way we can do this is with the spiritual practice of fasting.

Learning from Jesus

Before Jesus began his ministry, he was led into the wilderness by the Holy Spirit for a forty-day fast. As soon as his fast was over, Satan approached Jesus to tempt him. In his account of the story, Matthew makes sure to tell us that when Satan showed up, Jesus was hungry (Matt. 4:2). Often, I've seen different pastors and authors interpret this point in Jesus's life as him experiencing a moment of weakness. This perspective is understandable as a human body having gone without food for forty days is not going to be at prime condition. But Jesus's fast was meant to prepare him for ministry. While his physical body might have been weak, his spiritual resolve was strong.

So when Satan shows up to tempt him, Jesus is not confused. We see this clarity and resolve with the responses that he provides with each temptation. As the enemy tempts him to consume power, food, and prestige, we see Jesus respond by reciting the Scriptures. He pushes back the enemy with the words of God. Jesus's response to the enemy communicates that he was convinced that what God has to offer is better than what the world could provide.

A Spiritual Palate Cleanser

At its core, fasting is self-denial. But more than that, it's an expression that our greatest pleasure and satisfaction are found in God. This practice helps us remember that while food sustains our bodies, God sustains our souls. When we intentionally empty ourselves, we make room for God to fill us in ways we might not have expected.

I see fasting as a spiritual palate cleanser. By voluntarily giving up something—usually food—we experience a physical hunger that awakens our spiritual hunger. Often this is because during these moments of physical hunger we are connecting with God in prayer, and something supernatural happens in those prayers! The intimacy we develop with God during this time starts to break us free from being consumed with the things of the world. As our spiritual eyes are opened, the temptations of culture gradually lose their luster. Rather than being enticed by the shiny lights of TV advertisements or social media influencers, we see them for what they really are—distractions that provide momentary shots of joy.

Fasting helps us to train our hearts and minds to believe that true joy comes from this deeper intimacy with God. Moreover, instead of trying to manufacture it, we realize that joy already exists in our life as the Holy Spirit highlights the overflow of God's goodness that we have been given. Slowly, over time, this truth transforms us into people who are grateful and content. Even in life experiences that are hard or heartbreaking, we become people who first look to God to soothe our pain, not his creation.

In our world, there is no opting out of formation. We either opt into being formed by our culture or opt into being formed by Christ. Fasting empowers us to resist the pull of our culture as we opt into being formed by our Savior. It is a gift that helps us learn that the long and lasting joy our hearts desire only comes from one Source—God.

Living It Out

The false story whispered all around you is this: "Overconsumption leads to joy." But the true story sings a different tune: "No—communion with God leads to joy." You likely already desire to break free from the former in favor of the latter, but the jump from *desiring* this to *doing* it is simply a matter of habit—the habit of fasting.

And so, I want to challenge you: This week, mark a time period on your calendar, and fast from something that you'd typically consume without thinking, or something you regularly consider a source of joy. It may be some type of food or drink for a week. It may be social media for a month. It may be refraining from hitting "buy" within the app of your favorite retailer for a few months, only purchasing things you need in a store down the street. It may be abstaining from a certain kind of show or movie for half a year—you know, whatever reruns or binge-episodes you watch to feel some sort of spark of happiness before you go to bed.

I don't know the specifics of what God might be asking you to give to him for a season, but I know this: He is the true Source of all joy, and the gospel work of Jesus gave you access to that Source at great cost to himself. Why not, armed with this new habit, run toward the better story and the better Source of joy?

Chapter 6

A Better Hope

As I've gotten older, the conversations I have with my friends have changed. There are still plenty of conversations about the joys of life, work stress, and the takeout we are ordering for dinner. But now, conversations about death have been added to this list. Over the past few years, I have seen the number of conversations I've had about it increase. This is because my friends are starting to lose their parents or other loved ones from their parents' generation. Recently, I had to watch my cousins bury their mom and my best friend bury her dad. Honestly, those moments were heartbreaking. The older I get, death never gets easier to deal with. It has always been an unwanted reality, and I still feel that way about it.

Since those close to me know the losses I've experienced, they tend to come find me when they are experiencing similar losses of their own. This happened recently as a friend texted me to let me know she thought her dad was dying. He had been battling cancer for a while and the end-of-life signs were starting to show. During our conversation she asked me an honest and vulnerable question: "Elizabeth, how do I pray?"

My friend wanted to pray for healing while also staying in line with God's will. In her mind, if God's will wasn't to heal her dad on this side of eternity, she didn't want to go against that. But since it was her dad, she longed to have more time with him.

You might disagree, but I believe that in our most vulnerable moments, we don't have to do the heavy work of being super clear in our prayer because the Holy Spirit intercedes for us when we don't have the words to speak (Rom. 8:26–27). God understands the deep love we have for our family and friends, is present with us in the pain, and understands our desire to hold onto them just a little bit longer. We don't have to give up hope to honor his will. Or to put it in the biblical terms of 1 Corinthians 13:7 and 1 Peter 2:17, it is possible to "hope all things" and "fear" God at the same time.

So I told my friend to pray for her dad's healing with open hands, knowing God might heal on this side of eternity or the next. I also told her to hold onto the hope that God would do it on this side until he showed her otherwise.

While we can navigate life without having peace, make do as we struggle to find our identity, and take time to forgive someone who has wronged us, we don't do too well without hope. Hopelessness is an emotional virus that sucks the life out of us until we no longer believe it's worth living. I've seen what it can do to many people, especially a dear friend who ended her own life because her hopelessness was too much to bear.

Life can get chaotic. Sometimes it takes away our peace due to relational strife or conflict at work. But there are some situations that go beyond the normal level of difficulty. They weigh on us for months, if not years, as we wrestle with the possibility that our situation will never get better or easier. Perhaps we feel deep grief as we watch a loved one's health decline, or we look up and realize that decades have passed and our life is nowhere near where we wanted it to be. Maybe we've gotten ourselves into a predicament where we feel stuck—stuck in a loveless marriage, stuck in a sick body, or stuck in financial debt that feels impossible to repay.

Hopelessness makes these situations unbearable. Like a prisoner who is chained to an iron ball, we are struggling to crawl just a few feet because the weight is too great. Hope, on the other hand, makes hard situations not only bearable, but gives us a positive disposition that makes us seem a bit delusional. It will lead us to walk around with a smile on our face while our life is on fire. And, when people ask us why we are not freaking out, hope helps us respond with the simple phrase, "God will work it out somehow."

Simply put, to survive in this sin infected world, we need hope. And, like the other core desires we've talked about, hope is a gift God has been giving to his children for a long time.

Back to the Beginning

After their act of disobedience, Adam and Eve are promptly evicted from the garden. To prevent them from eating from the tree of life, God sent them out of Eden to work the ground from which they were taken. Scripture does not give us much detail about where Adam and Eve were headed, except to say they went east of Eden. Scripture doesn't specify whether they were heading anywhere in particular or simply wandering, making the best out of a bad situation.

I can't imagine what that must have been like for them. To have lived alongside the glory of God in a paradise and then to be stripped of your garden privileges and kicked out with no chance of ever returning to what you had lost. Nevertheless, God was gracious to them. God did not kill them on the spot after their disobedience, granting them a gracious eviction instead. Furthermore, God's grace didn't stay in the garden, it went with them.

Before the eviction, God makes garments for Adam and Eve to replace their fig leaves. He knew their fig leaves would be an insufficient form of clothing, so he took the initiative to give them better ones. He makes a sacrifice from one of his other created beings to help prepare them for the world they are about to enter. Moreover, in Genesis 4, after they have left Eden, we learn that Adam and Eve had two sons—Cain and Abel. We also read about how these men presented sacrifices to God. When Cain's sacrifice was not accepted, God talked to him about it. Wait? What?! This detail can be passed over easily. Even though God kicked humanity out of his paradise because of their sin, he is still showing up in their lives.

I am a visual person, so I think in pictures. The picture that has always come to mind about the end of Genesis 3 is God standing at the door of Eden watching Adam and Eve walk away till they no longer could be seen in the distance. To be kicked out of Eden is to be completely cut off from proximity and relationship with God, right? Apparently not.

Before and after their exit, God extends grace to his first humans. He gives them provisions for their trip and then continues to provide his presence. Even though they disobeyed, God sticks with them. This grace is the first glimmer of a promise God made in Genesis 3:15. When he cursed the serpent, God said, "I will put hostility between you and the woman, and between your offspring and her offspring. He will strike your head, and you will strike his heel." A strike to the head is fatal; a strike to the heel is not. In this verse, God promises that the offspring of the woman will one day conquer the enemy and enact justice for his rebellion against God.

As we walk through the rest of the biblical story, we'll come to learn that the "offspring" God is talking about is his Son, Jesus. But between this point and the coming of Jesus, God doesn't wander off. He sticks with his creation, making sure they stay on track to reach the point of restoration. With another sacrifice, he will restore humanity's relationship with him for eternity.

When I think back to the garments God made for Adam and Eve and how he shows up in the life of Cain and Abel, I see these as glimmers of hope—small nuggets in the story that point us to the greater truth that God hasn't stepped away from his human experiment, but somehow, some way, he will work it out. This same hope anchors us as God's presence in our life reminds us that no matter what happens, he'll work it out for us too.

But holding onto this hope requires that we face the reality of our dire circumstances, and that is not easy, especially when the world presents us with a smorgasbord of options that are designed to help us forget.

Our Culture's Story: *Avoid the Pain with Escapism*

My Christmas usually involves watching Christmas movies with my family. My mother likes watching classic movies, like *It's a Wonderful Life* or *A Christmas Carol*. Every so often, she'll find a modern remake of a classic movie and save it for me to watch when I come home. This past Christmas we watched a modern take on *A Christmas Carol* called *A Stone Cold Christmas*. By the name alone, I knew the movie was going to be very entertaining!

If you are unfamiliar with *A Christmas Carol*, it tells the story of a cold-hearted man named Ebenezer Scrooge. One night, Scrooge is visited by ghosts who show him what will happen if he doesn't change his stingy, mean ways. The same thing happens to the main star of the remake I watched with my mom. But, instead of agreeing to cooperate with the ghost (which is understandable because who would do that?!), she tries to run away from him.

In a dream, she first sees him following her home one night. She runs home and locks the door. But he ends up still getting in. Next, she gets into a car and sees that the ghost is the driver. She promptly gets out, runs back into her house and hides under a table. This dance between her and the ghost goes on for some time, and with each escape she believes she has gotten away from him. But each time, she soon realizes he is still there.

In moments of prolonged difficulty, many of us respond like the woman in the movie. Instead of facing our problems, we try to run away from them. We take one of the many escape routes our culture provides with the hope that when we get to "safety" our problems won't be there.

The desire to escape is a universal experience. In Rush Witt's book *I Want to Escape*, he provides a framework for human habits that will be especially helpful for our conversation about escapism. Here are the four categories he says our escape routes lead us to:

Denial: Toxic Positivity

Sometimes our escape route of choice is denial, ignoring the issue and acting like everything is okay. While we can have a positive attitude in the midst of a valley season, that positivity (which is different from biblical hope) can be fueled by our refusal to acknowledge the reality of our situation. It reminds me of the popular meme with the dog that's standing in front of a massive fire who's saying, "I'm fine, everything is fine!" Instead of acknowledging the depth of our pain or difficulties, denial leads us to minimize them or change the subject when asked about them. If we just put on a happy face and white-knuckle it through the situation, everything will work out.

Distraction: Social Media

Instead of denying our situation, sometimes we'll escape by actively forgetting about it. One of the easiest ways to do this is by logging on to social media and accessing an endless supply of videos that perfectly fit our interests. Whether you love crocheting, cooking, parenting hacks, work-out tips, fashion, or viral dances, with the touch of a finger you can stay entertained for hours.

However, these videos don't require us to engage our critical thinking skills. So much so, that it feels like social media almost transports you into another world where you check your brain at the door. Every time you log on to an app and start scrolling, it's as if you leave your reality and get to exist separate from your problems and responsibilities. This new world presents itself as a harmless place to hide from your problems while having fun!

Destruction: Rage and Isolation

In the words of Rush Witt, "When life overwhelms, growing anxieties often lead us into a destructive panic. . . . When we feel cornered by life, our hearts tend to lurch out in destructive ways and words."[1] This destruction can be loud, as when we burst out in anger at a family member or coworker. Instead of addressing the problem, we direct our rage at the people who are around us the most. We might even become highly critical of everyone and everything, making ourselves feel better by tearing down those around us.

Other times the destruction is silent as we withdraw from people. Instead of finding solace in community, we find it by being alone. But this isn't a silent retreat or weekend getaway. Over time, we stop talking to family and friends, and make a home in our makeshift solitary confinement.

Death: Suicide

If left unattended for too long, feelings of despair and disappointment can lead us to believe that there is no end in sight to our pain. However, the idea of having to carry our pain for an indefinite period of time becomes more than unbearable. Sadly, it becomes the fuel by which we start to contemplate leaving this world to be with God. Death seems to be the only glimmer of hope for a moment free of the pain we've been carrying for so long.

Formed by Culture

The link between all these behaviors is that they *seem* to be effective ways to relieve the despair and disappointment we are feeling. We just want to feel good. For the moment, toxic positivity feels good, watching mindless TikTok videos feels good, letting off some steam with a few sharp words feels good, and unfortunately, for some, the thought of ending our pain by ending our life feels good. But these "good" feelings don't last for long. Furthermore, our passive behavior is not without consequence. Like weeds in a garden, our unattended problems have most likely continued to grow, and our escapism has detrimentally impacted us and the people around us.

Let's just think about something as simple as watching one too many viral videos. While these provide a convenient distraction, they are not harmless. This is because social media apps are created by companies that have an economic interest in keeping us online. Using strategic design elements, they have found powerful ways to grab our attention and hold it.

Slowly, over time, these programs have formed us in such a way that the more we use them the more difficult it becomes to turn them off.

Unbeknownst to us, by accepting their invitation to escape for a few moments of mindless entertainment, we are likely to develop an addiction that will negatively impact our minds.[2] Studies show the constant stream of dopamine-filled distraction hits are reducing our attention spans and ability to focus.[3] This has resulted in a reduced capacity for reading long-form writing (i.e., books or articles), attention in our relationships (i.e., with our children), and FOMO that makes it hard for us to be present because we feel the pull to constantly check in on what other people are doing.

Or think about the power of anger. Rage suffocates relationships, leaving people on edge not knowing when they will meet your verbal wrath. Some loving friends might try to talk to us about it, but many will tell us with their feet, distancing themselves from us. If our anger is taken out on a spouse, child, or family member, it has the power to do even more damage, since these relationships are often more intimate. Also, since our family cannot always distance themselves from us physically, the distancing is done emotionally. Each harsh word and angry outburst dissolves the bonds of trust, safety, and vulnerability that help relationships thrive.

Whether they fall into the category of denial, distraction, destruction or death, our habits of escapism are telling us a faulty story and will continue to wreak havoc on our lives until we decide to stop listening. But once we do, we'll see that even though we've been running for a long time—similar to the woman in the movie—our problems are still right behind us.

God's Story: *Face the Pain with Truth*

If there is a moment in the life of Israel when it feels like they have hit rock bottom, it is when God sends them into exile. For generations Israel's kings led the people to worship idols, disobey the covenant, and ignore the prophets God sent to bring them back to the path of obedience and holiness. Eventually, in a tragic form of "tough love," God allows Israel to experience the consequences of their actions. He allows the pagan nation Babylon to attack them and take them from Jerusalem to Babylon in captivity. It was a long walk into exile, one that was hundreds of miles long.

During this season of exile, God didn't leave his people. He still spoke to them through his prophets, like the prophet Jeremiah. There is one piece of wisdom this prophet gave in Jeremiah 29:11 that is quite popular: "For I know the plans I have for you"—this is the Lord's declaration—"plans for your well-being, not for disaster, to give you a future and a hope." This verse is very encouraging, but its encouragement level skyrockets when you realize that this message of hope was given when Israel was hundreds of miles away from home in Babylonian captivity. Furthermore, when false prophets were tempting Israel to believe that they were going home immediately, Jeremiah's famous words come after his message that they would not go home for seventy years.

Through Jeremiah, God was giving Israel a hope to keep them, and anticipation of a greater day that would hold them tightly in the middle of their chaotic present circumstances. One day, God would fulfill the promises he had made to Israel's forefathers—Abraham, Moses, and David (Genesis 12; 15; 17; Exodus 20; 2 Samuel 7). In spite of their sin, weakness, or inadequacies, God would be faithful to finish what he began when he called Abraham, and when he brought humanity into existence. His promises of redemption were both temporal and eternal. In the same way that God had been faithful to Israel before, they could trust that he would be faithful once again. Instead of avoiding their pain, Jeremiah encouraged Israel to face it by remembering the truth of God's promises.

Moreover, even though their situation of difficulty was going to last longer than they hoped for, Jeremiah did not leave them to figure out how to pass the time. In the verses that precede the declaration of hope, Jeremiah instructs Israel to live with an intentionality that includes both celebration and cultivation. By building houses, gardens, and families, they were to invest in their current situation with a boldness that was fueled by a future hope rooted in God's past promises. Even though their season had changed, the mission God called them to had not. So while they waited, they were supposed to be fruitful. It's as if, because of God's consistent track record, Jeremiah was calling them to live as if what they hoped for was already realized. Their deeply rooted hope empowered them to live with boldness and purpose as they waited for God to be faithful once again.

Formed by God

In my early years of ministry, I found myself at a crossroads. I was in a job I loved but could not afford to keep. I had a roommate, but still my salary did not give me enough to pay my half of the rent. After much prayer, I believed God told me to humble myself and rent a room in the house of a family friend. But to do so, I would have to sell most of my belongings. I didn't have the money to store it or the money to move it. There was nowhere for it to go, except to the donation center.

I remember when the people from Goodwill showed up to get my stuff. I think they were a little surprised that I was giving my couch, bed, and a few other nice items away. As they tried to politely probe for the reasons, I kindly kept them focused on their task because I didn't have words to communicate how low I felt. Never in my career did I think I would get to this moment. I never imagined that I would be stuffing most of my belongings into a small storage unit and putting the rest in my car to take to a room I'd be living in for the next six months. To add fuel to the fire, I had a few other personal issues going on that were bringing me even lower. To say that I was in a sad place would have been an understatement.

Surprisingly, after a few months, I was able to secure another job. With my new salary, I could afford to live in my own apartment again. About a month before I moved into my new apartment, I stayed with another friend who lived near my work. Before I moved out, she blessed me with all the furniture in the bedroom I had been using during my time with her. I remember standing in my new apartment that had fresh paint, new carpet, and hardly any furniture, the majority of which was given to me by my friend.

I currently still have a few of those furniture pieces, and every time I see them, I'm reminded of God's faithfulness. When I gave away all my furniture that day, I didn't know how God would help me get back on my feet. I just wanted to be obedient to his direction even though I didn't know what my obedience would cost me. But, in his grace and through the kindness of my friend, he helped to restore some of the things I had given up in my lowest moments. The furniture serves as a physical "stone of remembrance" that reminds me anything is possible with God. But it's not a reminder that just makes me feel all warm and fuzzy on the inside. It's a reminder that leads me to action—to hold out hope that God could do something restorative for me all over again, in a new season, if I genuinely needed him to. I am quick to move in faith, even if that means I must sacrifice something that's important to me, because I have seen with my own eyes that God is faithful to restore.

The history of God's work in our lives serves as a testament to what he will do for us in the future. With each answered prayer, point of provision, or miracle, we are shown once again that the God who has been with his people from the very beginning is still with us. When our culture's best answer to pain is to deny, destroy, or self-destruct, God's continued faithfulness to us produces an unshakable hope that sustains us and helps us persevere through pain instead. This gives us an assurance that he will show up and work out our situation. We may not know when or how, but we do know confidently that our faithful God will show up to save his people—because that's what he always does.

Habit of Resistance | Meditation

Our culture's false story of hope through avoidance encourages us to process our hopelessness through denial, distraction, or destruction. But, while those options might temporarily relieve our pain, the root issue still remains. On the other hand, God's story leads us to find hope through God's past faithfulness, because if he has been faithful before, we can be confident he will be again. In order to hold onto this hope, we must intentionally and actively remember what's true about God so these truths can come back to our minds and hearts in the moments we need them the most. The habit that will help us do this is *meditation*.

Learning from Jesus

The first few verses of Matthew 11 are ones I have come back to often in my own seasons of hopelessness. This portion of Matthew's Gospel tells the story of a conversation between John the Baptist and Jesus. John the Baptist was Jesus's cousin, born about six months before him. He dedicated his life to preparing the way for Jesus, inviting people to repent of their sins because the kingdom of heaven had come near (Matt. 3:2; Isa. 40:3). John had spent his entire life preparing for and preaching about the Messiah. However, his ministry work eventually led to his arrest and imprisonment.

Like all of us, John probably had expectations about his life. Perhaps he had expectations about the joy and excitement of doing ministry alongside the Messiah. He had grown up hearing about his cousin, about the angel that visited Jesus's mother and father, and the miraculous way the God of the universe chose to make his appearance on earth. But joy and excitement have a way of disappearing when the difficulties of life have stayed with us too long. This was the case for John, because when his storyline picks back up in Matthew 11, he isn't preparing the way for Jesus anymore. He's questioning whether his cousin is really the Messiah.

Having heard about all the miracles Jesus was doing for everyone but him, John sends a message to Jesus through his disciples in verse 3: "Are you the one who is to come, or should we expect someone else?" Only a few chapters earlier, Matthew tells us about how John baptized Jesus! It is one of few moments in Scripture where the entire Godhead is present—God the Father, God the Son, and God the Holy Spirit! But some time has passed since this event, and John's present situation leads him to doubt.

I find myself returning to this passage often partly because of the humanity of John's question. He didn't expect his life to go the way it had, and those unmet expectations were causing him to struggle. However, I also find myself deeply encouraged by Jesus's response. First, Jesus doesn't chastise John for his doubt. He doesn't belittle him or question his loyalty. He has space for the messiness of John's life. Second, Jesus doesn't respond directly. He doesn't say something like, "Hey, John, I'm sorry things haven't been going well for you. I planned on coming to visit but . . ." Instead, Jesus responds by quoting Old Testament Scripture:

> Jesus replied to them, "Go and report to John what you hear and see: The blind receive their sight, the lame walk, those with leprosy are cleansed, the deaf hear, the dead are raised, and the poor are told the good news, and blessed is the one who isn't offended by me." (Matt. 11:4–6)

With these words, Jesus references multiple passages from the same book—Isaiah 8:14–15; 26:18–19; 29:18–19; 35:5–6; 53:4; and 61:1. Each of these passages are prophecies about what the Messiah will do when he comes and how those who don't believe in him will respond to his ministry. Isaiah is full of prophecies about the Messiah. As a Jewish man, John would have recognized these passages because he would have studied them growing up. Jesus knew this. So when he points John back to Isaiah, Jesus is using the fruit of his ministry to affirm that he is the Messiah.

However, Jesus is also doing something else. In a moment when John is struggling to find hope, Jesus reminds him of the truths he had learned years before.

Building a Foundation

Pam and Warren Adams are a couple who lived near Galveston, Texas. They loved living near the water, even though their region was often frequented by hurricanes. In

2005, a hurricane came through their area and demolished their home. Since the Adams loved living there so much, they decided to rebuild. Instead of building their house fourteen feet above sea level like last time, this time they built it up twenty feet.

Three years later another hurricane came through. Like the last time, they evacuated and waited for the announcement that it was safe for them to come home. Once it was safe, they returned to a scene similar to the destruction of the 2005 hurricane. There was devastation everywhere. There was a clear eye line to the shore because every house had been fully demolished. Well, every house but one. The Adams house was the only one left standing.

One thing that stood out to me when I first heard this story is what Pam and Warren *weren't* doing when the second evacuation alarm went off. They weren't going to Home Depot to buy cement or looking through the phone book for a contractor to make emergency improvements to their house. All the work to improve their foundation had been done before the storm came. With each day of construction, they took the time, made the plans, invested the money, and put in the work to strengthen their home's foundation. And when the storm came, all that investment helped to save their home.

The Adam's story reminds me of the power of building a foundation to help us weather storms of hopelessness. One way we can do this is by following Jesus's words to John—meditating on the truth of Scripture. Specifically, we need to meditate on the promises of God. Scripture is full of hundreds of promises that help remind us of the character and commitments of God. Furthermore, we know that God makes good on his promises because he is faithful. Instead of using our culture's escape routes to try to run away from our problems, we can use the Word of God to help us face them with hope. No matter the situation, there is nothing in this world that is a match for the power of God. In the words of Jonathan, "Nothing can keep the LORD from saving, whether by many or by few" (1 Sam. 14:6).

When hopelessness has us believing the lie that we don't matter, Ephesians 2:10 reminds us that God created us for good works which he prepared beforehand for us to do. When it tempts us to believe the lie that in a dark night of the soul we are alone, Psalm 139 reminds us that in the darkness God is there, for the darkness is not dark to him. And when it tempts us to believe the lie that we have to get out of our mess on our own, Philippians 1:6 reminds us that he who began a good work in us will carry it on until the day of completion in Christ Jesus.

When hopelessness tempts us with any lie, the promises of Scripture help us fight back and resist their pull. However, even though we can Google the promises of God or ask a friend to send us an encouraging verse when times are hard, we can also prepare for the storm in seasons when the light of hope is shining bright. When we meditate on God's Word, taking time to study it, pray it, read it slowly over and over again, we are laying stones in the foundation of our spiritual house. And one day this foundation will help us fight back against hopelessness—like Jesus, we'll look back to the truth we've learned to remember where true hope can be found.

Another way we can strengthen our "foundation" is by remembering the faithfulness of God in our own lives. When we remember, specifically what God has done in the past, we are able to have hope that our future will be characterized by this same goodness (Ps. 77:11–12). We can find a beautiful example of this in Psalm 77. The psalmist begins by sharing about his moment of crisis and his doubts about God's character and promises. But a shift happens in verse 11. The psalmist encourages himself by looking to the past deeds of God. He says, "I will remember the Lord's works; yes, I will remember your ancient wonders. I will reflect on all you have done and meditate on your actions." For the rest of psalm, he recounts God's work in the world, both in creation and in the life of Israel. As you read the words, you can feel his countenance lift. The doubt and despair start to fade into the background as the faithfulness of God takes center stage.

The more you talk about God's past deeds, the more your hope is bolstered, because if God has been faithful before, he will surely be faithful again.

Live It Out

Our culture's false story sounds like this: "You can find hope by escaping. If you ignore your problems through distraction, denial, or destructive tendencies, you won't have to face hard things." While this might sound alluring, this story fails to tell you that you can never outrun hopelessness, and eventually the problems you are trying to escape or avoid will find you again.

On the other hand, God's story offers us a better option: "You can find hope by trusting in God's faithfulness. By remembering his words and his actions, your hope is bolstered to believe that if God has been faithful before, he will surely be faithful again." To go from one story to the other requires the habit of meditation, which helps us train our minds to choose a different thought pathway when confronted with the challenging reality of our current situation. Instead of running from pain, we can face it as we measure it against the greatness of God, discovering once again that God is greater.

To help you lean into a habit of meditation, I want to challenge you to do two things:

1. First, create a list entitled "Where I'm Asking God to Show Up for Me." On this list, write down the things you are worried about. It might be something related to your job, a family member, or a fear you have about the future. Next to each worry, write a verse or passage from Scripture that details what God can do or has already done in the situation. Use this list in your time of prayer, recounting to God what his Word says.

    "Lord, in ______________, you said
    that you would ________________.
    Please be faithful to do this in my life."

2. Next, create a second list entitled "Where God Has Already Showed Up for Me." Spend some time thinking about the ways God has shown up in your life over the past few weeks, months, and years. Remember the ways he answered prayers, provided tangibly for your needs, and the miracles he might have even brought your way. As each occurrence comes to mind, write it down. Pay attention to how your countenance changes from the time you started writing till the moment you finish. Hopefully, like the psalmist in Psalm 77, you'll have a bit more hope as the past actions of God are brought to the forefront of your mind.

Schedule a regular time to return to these two lists. Maybe it is once a week during your prayer time or you could get your friends and family involved by practicing it corporately once a month over a meal. The more often the better, because the more we remember the faithfulness of God, the easier it is to persevere in an in-between season. Even if we might not be clear on how our situation will resolve, the habit of meditation helps grow our confidence that God knows and, at the right time, he will provide, sustain, and get us to the place we need to be.

Chapter 7

A Better Gospel

Every so often, I visit my sister for an "Auntie Liz Weekend." This is when I babysit my two nephews for a few days, so my sister and her husband can get away for a short couple's vacation. Auntie Liz weekends are driven by two principles—survival and fun! No one is forced to eat vegetables, we will probably consume more sweets than we should, and we'll play lots of games, watch movies, and have plenty of snuggle time! While there will be a few rules everyone has to follow, my goal is not to be a disciplinarian, but simply to make sure everyone, including myself, makes it through the weekend alive!

During my inaugural Auntie Liz weekend, I remember the conversation I had with my youngest nephew, who at the time was four years old. With eloquence and confidence, he tried to tell me why I didn't need to help him get ready for bed. In his mind, he had rationalized why he could do his bedtime routine on his own, without any assistance. He was going to take his shower, brush his teeth, and get dressed for bed all on his own, without my supervision. As I graciously indulged him in conversation, it became clear that my nephew's ideas were motivated by the desire to do things his way. He wanted the freedom to do whatever he wanted, and had a strong belief that his way was the best way.

Now, it's good for kids to grow in their ability to perform everyday chores and household practices—learning to do these things is part of growing up. However, his limited life experience prevented him from seeing that his desire for complete autonomy would not produce the results he believed it would. I knew that most—or even none—of the things he had listed would happen if he had zero supervision. Rather, I would likely return to his room to find him the same way I left him, playing with one of his favorite toys. Even worse, if he had actually tried to tackle all those tasks on his own without any guidance, he could have gotten seriously hurt. Something as simple as using a new shower with different hardware and hotter water than he was used to could have burned him in an instant.

The real issue wasn't that he wanted to learn new things or grow more confident in his skills; that part was good. The problem was that he wanted to do it all without any authority or oversight. He wanted total autonomy—to be free of me.

Reflecting on this conversation, I'm pretty sure I was doing my best to not laugh while my nephew pontificated about his seemingly ingenious plan. But even though the details of the plan might have been new to me, his confidence and desire for total independence was not. It felt familiar. I knew what it was like to do my best to convince someone that a bad plan—especially with no supervision or authority involved—was good.

I'm more than sure I did this with my own parents, but I also know I've done it in my conversations with God.

But I'm not alone in this. You've done it too, because as humans we all share several common traits and one of them is a love of *freedom*.

Perhaps this love of freedom is simply a universal, human thing. No one likes to be coerced. Even when it happens in small or subtle ways, everyone can feel when they are being situationally pinned down, backed into a corner, or forced into a plan they aren't on board with. Or maybe the version of freedom you and I tend to prize most is an American thing, due to our country's historical backstory and original intent for all men to be free—a value that has deeply shaped us, even though it hasn't always been applied equally.[1] The truth is, it's probably a mixture of both.

Widespread and well-embraced as this value is, freedom is a tricky concept because its definition has evolved in recent decades. What individual freedom meant at the time of our country's founding—and what the concept of freedom truly requires no matter what country or environment it finds itself—is not what our culture means by freedom now. While versions of freedom in history have traditionally meant to "pursue our own wellbeing within the limits and constraints that make up the created order,"[2] it now means being able to do whatever your instincts tell you with zero limitations, constraints, supervision, or authority. It's not just autonomy; it's autonomy with no authority, accountability, restraints, or care for the common good. It's unbridled, unchecked, and unquestionable decision-making for the individual over and against any thought for the greater community. Here's how Trevin Wax puts it:

> The old way of thinking . . . was about the freedom to make your way in the world, to pursue "the good life" without being hindered by too many governmental restrictions as you sought to become a whole and flourishing person who contributes to your community. The new way of thinking . . . is about the freedom to buck the community's consensus, to determine for yourself what "happiness" is, and then pursue personal freedom at all costs without submitting to any authority that might constrain your desires.[3]

In short, freedom these days is basically a four-year-old doing whatever he fancies with no oversight from any sort of adult. And like I said before, we all feel the pull of this new definition of freedom. There is a certain allure that comes with autonomy, especially when one has lived within a system without freedom. Rather than being hemmed in by boundaries and restrictions, freedom provides an open space for opportunity, discovery, and invention. It gives us permission to do what we please and relinquish anything that hinders our desires.

But unrestrained freedom isn't neutral; our experience of it is controlled by whoever is in the driver's seat of our lives.

Back to the Beginning

Throughout this book, we've spent a lot of time in the first few chapters of Genesis, looking anew at the creation story to glean new insights. You might be tired of talking about it, but please stick with me! There is one more observation I want us to think about. We have seen what life was like before and after the fall, but we haven't actually talked about what happened in that one moment that changed everything.

Hopefully, you've picked up on the fact that God designed humanity to flourish. The opening pages of Genesis describe how out of the overflow of his love, our triune God created a paradise for his creation to enjoy with him. The garden of Eden was an environment of shalom—peace, wholeness, and delight.[4] Or, as I defined it in the introduction of this book, *shalom is the good life.* It's a life *where everything is as it ought to be.* Eden came with only one constraint for Adam and Eve: Don't eat from the tree of the knowledge of good and evil. The whole garden was theirs and only one tree was off-limits.

Tempted by the serpent, Adam and Eve decide to trust their curiosity over the commands of God. By eating the fruit of the forbidden tree, they used their freedom to do the one thing God told them not to. This decision to disobey God was not inconsequential. God, the Creator of the universe, is the one in control. It is his world they live in, his kingdom they occupy. Instead of following God as their King, they usurp his authority. In the words of Desmond Alexander, "By betraying God and obeying the serpent, the royal couple dethrone God. . . . The ones through whom God's sovereignty was to be extended throughout the earth side with his enemy. By heeding the serpent they not only give it control over the earth, but they themselves become its subjects."[5]

Adam and Eve had committed cosmic treason. In their disobedience, they positioned themselves as rivals to the one true King. They chose to live by their own law, rather than by God's law. They sought total autonomy without constraints in a world that God has created and sustains.[6]

Adam and Eve's choice to live outside of the rule of God is the first time we see humans attempting to live in unrestrained autonomy in the biblical narrative. However, instead of using the phrase "unrestrained autonomy" to describe Adam and Eve's actions, Scripture uses the word *sin*. As the story of the Bible unfolds, we learn how sin destroys shalom. As humans choose their own way, pursuing a mutant version of freedom that is rooted in the elevation of self over God, we create a world that moves farther and farther away from how things were supposed to be. Sin leads us away from the perfect peace, love, joy, and hope that God intended for us to have, and toward a place of brokenness.

God's commands were boundary lines, and any action out of these bounds would dishonor their Creator. When humanity lives within the lines, they flourish. I love how Tim Keller explains this: "In many areas of life, freedom is not so much the absence of restrictions as finding the right ones, the liberating restrictions. Those that fit the reality of our nature and the world produce greater power and scope for our abilities and a deeper joy and fulfillment."[7]

However, when Adam and Eve stepped outside of the box, the *perfect* state of their flourishing evaporated. God gifted humanity with a freedom that was inextricably linked to responsibility. What Adam and Eve realized in that fateful moment is that while they were free to choose, they could not control the consequences of their decisions.

Our Culture's Story: *Freedom of Expression*

We've already discussed how our culture currently defines freedom in a general sense. But there's a particular outworking of this definition that I'd like us to consider, and that's our love for *freedom of expression.* We enjoy being able to say whatever we want, however we want, to whomever we want. With pictures and words, we freely express our ideas and life experiences publicly. But as we share, we also scroll and comment on social media posts curated by an algorithm. These technologies control the results we get from our search engine inputs, the stories that show up in our news feed, and the social media posts that are pushed to us on our platform of choice. While we believe that we are consuming the information of our own choosing, we are actually consuming information that has been selected for us by these algorithms.

Eli Pariser calls this dynamic "filter bubbles."[8] In his book of the same name, Pariser describes how the personalization of the internet places us into invisible silos, creating a unique universe of information for us. Based upon data points that have been collected about us online, our silos filter information in and out. Impartial information seldom makes it into our filter bubbles. What this means is that the internet is showing us what it thinks we want to see, but not necessarily what we *need* to see.

Our "filter bubbles" tend to show us information that is shared by like-minded people. So if you are more progressive politically, it is unlikely that you will be shown posts, ads, or videos from your more conservative counterparts. Over time, this artificial grouping pulls us further and further away from people we are different from, whose ideas and life experiences challenge our own.

The more we post and scroll, the more we teach the algorithm our preferences. Since social media companies are invested in keeping us online, they will keep showing us what we want to see. So instead of giving us access to the entire world, our freedom of expression places us in an information silo and this perpetual place of disconnection makes it easy for us to see our fellow image-bearers as "other." They also make it easy for us to disregard the complexity of someone's humanity, ignoring the beauty in their differences. Instead, we see them as outside of our group, and once they no longer appear human in our eyes, we no longer feel the need to treat them as such.

Now, we might never say this out loud or vehemently argue otherwise. But think about it—why is it so easy for us to share vitriol online? Far too easily, comment sections can become dumpster fires, as with little hesitation people freely express opinions that most of them wouldn't have the courage to say in person. In the words of Felicia Su Wong, "Too often our digital practices make it easy for us to overlook the flickering holiness in other people."[9]

Moreover, the words we say are not without consequence. We've already explored how our meanness can fuel the merciless fires of cancel culture. However, our freedom of expression can rise to the level of online bullying which can have fatal consequences.[10] It can also be a breeding ground for misinformation, leading to conspiracy theories and impacting people's behavior offline.

Social media promises us free expression in a controlled environment. But the truth is that our ability to express ourselves is in large part influenced by tech companies. While much positivity is spread on these platforms, they are also a place where we become more and more comfortable with negativity, cynicism, fear, and a slew of other polarizing emotions that detrimentally impact others online and offline. In the end, sure, it's fine to have freedom of expression. That's important. But we're rewarded (in unprecedented ways) for that freedom and those expressions to be not only unkind, but unbridled and unrestrained—no matter the cost the common good has to pay and with no regard to any sort of authority who might ask us to express ourselves otherwise.

Formed by Culture

In each chapter of this book, we've taken time to examine different cultural stories that promise to fulfill our core desires but fall short. Hopefully, you've noticed that all these stories have one thing in common—they fuel our desire for unrestrained autonomy, the ability to do whatever we want to.

With creative and powerful messaging, they paint a seemingly beautiful vision about the potential of complete independence from any sort of authority. But, with all the effort that is used to spread this message, there is an even greater effort exerted to ensure we don't consider what it will cost us and others.

Tim Keller points out the first missing detail from our culture's message about freedom: "Even though you want to be free, you are not. You must live for something, and whatever it is will enslave you."[11] The cultural narrative might frame freedom as something exercised without any oversight or authority, but the notion of someone living with no authority involved in their daily choices is a myth. Whether it be our own internal (and ever-changing) desires dictating our every move or some other external influence bossing us around, everyone bows to some sort of ultimate authority. As the apostle Peter reminds us, "people are slaves to whatever has mastered them" (2 Pet. 2:19 NIV). And that's because as humans, we were created to follow. It's a part of our hard wiring. We will always have a master, enslaved to someone or something to find the fulfillment and satisfaction we need. The question is not *if* we are following some authority figure. It's *who*, or *what* exactly, we are choosing to follow. It's this: *What masters you*, and is that master good to you? Scripture recognizes this every time it talks about "two ways" or "two paths." Whether it's the way of wisdom and the way of folly in Proverbs or the narrow path and the wide path we read about in the Gospels, the Bible is clear that there are only two options in life. We can either follow the world or God.

The pervasive false stories in our culture continue to tempt us in the same way the serpent did in the garden. We're led to believe that we are missing out on something if we don't step outside of the boundaries God has created for us. Instead of trusting our Creator, we are encouraged to trust ourselves. But we are not immune to our environments; we don't live in a vacuum. Rather we are like sponges, absorbing the information that is presented around us, using it to determine how we are going to show up in the world. The beliefs, behaviors, and ideologies of whoever we are following shape what we think is a worthwhile use of our time, money, and resources.

Each culture throughout history faces unique temptations that resonate with them. These temptations are constantly changing, as our way of living and our environments change. It's why our current belief—that our greatest guide is our subjective self (emotions)—would have been preposterous to a previous generation who believed authority was found in scientific facts or some supreme spiritual being that controlled the world.[12]

The second missing detail from our culture's message about freedom is that by using their methods, we will inevitably exploit other people to get what we want.[13] Whether we like it or not, we are interconnected with the people around us. How we choose to live affects other people, which means our actions can be of benefit to them or detrimental.

Our selfish pursuit of unrestrained freedom will inevitably cause us to mistreat someone when they get in the way. We might dishonor people in our quest for selfish love, or heap shame on others who don't meet our standards for value and meaning. Perhaps this freedom might lead to something more insidious like an injustice we commit to hold onto our money or power. Or we might take something that doesn't belong to us, like a physical item or someone's sexuality, so that we can find pleasure. The list is endless of how we will exploit others, because if our desire for freedom is rooted in us, then we won't deny our own fleshly desires, even when they negatively impact someone else.

Sometimes people claim that using their freedoms however they choose is fine as long as it doesn't harm others. While this is a common rationale, there are two problems. First, "not harming someone" is a pretty low bar for how to use one's freedom in the world. It's a bare-minimum approach. Why settle for "I'll use my freedom in ways that don't harm others" when we could say "I'll use my freedom in ways that *love* others"? There is a world of difference between the two. To approach life with only the former in mind reveals how self-centered a person truly is. Sure, plenty of people can use the argument that they didn't do anything bad, per se, in many situations. But that sort of rationale only betrays the fact that they also didn't contribute anything good. Imagine a world where the only standard for using one's freedom is avoiding "bad," and no one uses their freedom to contribute anything *good*? It would be a pretty drab world. As the apostle Paul would say, "Don't use your freedom as an excuse to do anything you want. Use it as an opportunity to serve each other with love" (Gal. 5:13 CEV).

Second, people differ in their understanding of "harm," and what someone believes to be harmful you might not. In order for us to exist without chaos as a society, there has to be a shared standard of restriction—things we all agree are off-limits for all of us. Said another way, we need consensus on what constitutes harm. But in a culture where we all live by what feels true to us, who determines that standard? Who or what will we all agree to yield to when our ultimate authority is ourselves?

We are not free to do whatever we want. Like the tech companies that control the content we consume on our feeds, forming us to choose freedom of expression over kindness and respect, we are only free to do what our master beckons us to do.

The gospel of our culture leaves these details out, but the gospel of Christ does not.

God's Story: *Freedom of Self-Denial*

In Matthew 16, Jesus begins to share with his disciples the full extent of his kingdom mission. He tells them that he must go to Jerusalem, suffer, and be killed. He would then be raised from the dead on the third day. Hearing this, the disciples probably had a lot of thoughts running through their minds, but only one was courageous enough to share them. Upon hearing Jesus's announcement, Peter basically tells Jesus to chill out, saying "Oh no, Lord! This will never happen to you!" (Matt. 16:22).

Jesus's response to Peter is two-fold. First, he chastises Peter by saying, "Get behind me, Satan! You are a hindrance to me because you're not thinking about God's concerns but human concerns" (v. 23). Peter's misstep was rooted in his motivations. He tried to advance his own idea of what was right—instead of submitting to the plan of Jesus. His response was not in alignment with the mindset of a disciple, but someone who was in opposition to the things of God.

Next, since it seems like Peter has forgotten what it means to be a disciple, Jesus follows up with a quick discipleship lesson. He says, "If anyone wants to follow after me, let him deny himself, take up his cross, and follow me. For whoever wants to save his life will lose it, but whoever loses his life because of me will find it. For what will it benefit someone if he gains the whole world yet loses his life? Or what will anyone give in exchange for his life?" (vv. 24–26). With these words, Jesus reminds his disciples about the simple but challenging requirement of discipleship: self-denial.

Yet Jesus is not inviting us to do something that he himself has not done. His cross came *before* ours. He knows our experience of wholeness and delight can only come through our connection to God, because God is the ultimate and unending source of shalom. But since our sin has corrupted that connection, Jesus willingly took up a cross to restore it.

Jesus, the Son of God, came to earth as a man, using his freedom to be constrained within the limitations of this earthly world. His life and ministry were characterized by humility and obedience, even to the point of death (Phil. 2:5–8). Jesus suffered, died, and used his freedom for our sake. In contrast to a world that requires us to sacrifice ourselves for it, Jesus sacrificed himself for us. I love how Paul explains it in 2 Corinthians 5:21: "He made the one who did not know sin to be sin for us, so that in him we might become the righteousness of God."

Through Jesus's self-giving love we see how he is the better master, one who gives rather than takes. Instead of using his freedom for the bare minimum of "doing no harm," Jesus used his freedom in love for the greater good of all humanity. Instead of just seeking his personal gain or happiness, he surrendered his will to do the will of his Father so that we can experience an unending life of wholeness and delight (Luke 22:42).

Where the world's promises ultimately leave us enslaved to emptiness, Jesus's self-giving sacrifice provides us with a fullness of life beyond anything we can imagine. It is the eternal life, or the "abundant life" he mentions in John 10:10. It is the life we see breathed into all creation, the holistic peace we've been talking about. It is the flourishing we saw in Eden—the peace, love, joy, and perfect wholeness and harmony for which we were created.

Jesus makes it clear that we are unable to find life without him. Paradoxically, no matter how hard we work or what worldly benefits we accumulate, the life we desire will still evade us. In our attempts to hold onto our autonomy, we'll lose our life, never experiencing the good life on this side of eternity or the next. But if we give up our life and surrender our autonomy to the way of Jesus, we find it.

Contrary to what the world tells us, a life surrendered to Jesus is not a losing life; it is one of eternal gain.

Formed by God

One night a few months ago, I was searching for something to watch, and I came across a game show where 1,000 people were competing for five million dollars. The show seemed a bit unorthodox, with some contestant challenges that were both interesting and ethically questionable.

In the first episode, the host gave the contestants some unexpected challenges to help whittle down the contestant pool to 500 people. The contestants were arranged in a stadium in a grid pattern that had so many rows you couldn't see the people in the back from the front. One of the games required that one person in the row drop out to save everyone else on their row. There was a time limit to the game, so if someone didn't volunteer before time was up the entire row could be eliminated.

The stadium was full of cameras, so there was a ton of footage that showed the contestants struggling with the decision of whether to save their team. Some people refused to do it, but every so often you'd see a contestant give in and hit the button on a nearby stand that signaled they were dropping out. You could see the person crying, knowing they'd given up a chance at something big to help somebody else win. The contestants who had been saved also started crying, realizing a sacrifice had just been made on their behalf. They'd yell down the line to the person who gave up their spot, saying "I'm gonna win for you," "I won't forget you," or "I'm going to make it count!" With a lot of passion and tears, they were sharing their commitment to live differently. Their actions were going to be fueled by their gratitude for the gift they had received.

Sometimes, we can see God as a mean taskmaster, who is trying to ruin all the fun. Our culture hops onto this lie and tempts us to believe that following their pathway of freedom will help us experience all the goodness God wants to hide from us. But the gospel helps us see otherwise. It reminds us that goodness, wholeness of life, is only found through Jesus. And it is better than any counterfeit version we could get on our own. What we could not find on our own, by faith, Jesus makes available to us. He gave up his life for it, and the only response we ought to have is gratitude lived out through obedience. Just like the contestants in the show, Jesus's example of giving away his own freedom so that we might gain it also makes us desire to live differently.

This obedience does not earn our salvation or God's favor in our life. It also doesn't just relegate us to the back corner of God's presence where we get the crumbs from his table. No! By faith, our obedience reconnects us to the Source of shalom. So, as we walk in obedience, we walk in an overflow that doesn't just let us experience wholeness, but actually makes us whole.

As we walk according to the way of Jesus, we are transformed and re-formed. The ways of the world have formed us and given us a shell of sorts that blocks us from living out our divine design as image-bearers. By the power of the Holy Spirit this re-formation process helps us reclaim our divine identity and purpose as we grow to have lives that reflect the character of God and help cultivate a world where everyone flourishes and thrives. Instead of prioritizing our selfish desires and harming others, we prioritize others' desires and in doing so help them flourish. This is because we don't really have shalom individually unless we first have it corporately. Yes, we can have an individual experience of it in our relationship with Jesus. But it was meant to fill the world. It is the means through which we build families and cultivate our cities. In God's design, we all thrive when everyone is invested in everyone else's flourishing (Jer. 29:7).

So our obedience to God includes individual actions of personal holiness. But it also includes shalom restoration, as we seek to bring it to places where sin has eroded it. We may share it through serving the most vulnerable members of our society, using our economic overflow to invest in infrastructure to help our unhoused population. We might also share it with our voices by advocating for those who are experiencing injustice, or by showing care for someone whose personhood has been violated by human trafficking or domestic violence.

The opportunities to share what we've received are endless. And, these actions, alongside our commitment to godly character and spiritual fruitfulness are how we live in gratitude for the gift of peace, wholeness, and delight we've received. Because if we receive it only to hoard it for ourselves or those we deem worthy, then we've missed the point. We receive the gift of flourishing in part to give it away to others, as we wait for the One who gave it to us to return.

Habit of Resistance | A Rule of Life

We've spent much of our time examining the first few chapters of Genesis. This is because the beginning of the biblical story matters. The Bible does not start with sin but with our triune God creating an earthly paradise so he might dwell with his creation. I want to conclude by fast-forwarding to the end of the story, where we see how God will recreate what he made in the beginning.

Learning from Jesus

Revelation is a book that scares a lot of people. It is full of symbolism that can be hard to understand, especially if you are unfamiliar with the books of the Bible that precede it. However, it was not given to God's people to evoke fear, rather it was written to give us hope. A revelation of Jesus Christ that was given by an angel to the apostle John, the book of Revelation helps God's people know that even though there is a cosmic battle raging between God's kingdom and the kingdom of darkness, God *will* win.

My favorite passage in Revelation describes what life will be like after Christ returns and all the enemies of God are no more. In Revelation 21, John tells us:

> Then I saw a new heaven and a new earth; for the first heaven and the first earth had passed away, and the sea was no more. I also saw the holy city, the new Jerusalem, coming down

out of heaven from God, prepared like a bride adorned for her husband.

Then I heard a loud voice from the throne: Look, God's dwelling is with humanity, and he will live with them. They will be his peoples, and God himself will be with them and will be their God. He will wipe away every tear from their eyes. Death will be no more; grief, crying, and pain will be no more, because the previous things have passed away.

Then the one seated on the throne said, "Look, I am making everything new." He also said, "Write, because these words are faithful and true." Then he said to me, "It is done! I am the Alpha and the Omega, the beginning and the end. I will freely give to the thirsty from the spring of the water of life. The one who conquers will inherit these things, and I will be his God, and he will be my son. But the cowards, faithless, detestable, murderers, sexually immoral, sorcerers, idolaters, and all liars—their share will be in the lake that burns with fire and sulfur, which is the second death." (vv. 1–8)

* * *

I did not see a temple in it, because the Lord God the Almighty and the Lamb are its temple. The city does not need the sun or the

> moon to shine on it, because the glory of God illuminates it, and its lamp is the Lamb. The nations will walk by its light, and the kings of the earth will bring their glory into it. Its gates will never close by day because it will never be night there. They will bring the glory and honor of the nations into it. Nothing unclean will ever enter it, nor anyone who does what is detestable or false, but only those written in the Lamb's book of life. (vv. 22–27)

Hopefully, after reading those verses you can see why I love this passage. In these verses John describes the re-creation of Eden, which is the new Jerusalem. The paradise God created in the very beginning is not forever lost; he has recreated it for humanity. The perfect delight and harmony that existed in the beginning between God and all of creation is not erased from human history; it exists once again for eternity. The glory of God shines so bright that it provides a permanent light to the city, and its gates never close because there is nothing dark, sinful, or evil we need protection from.

The plurality of the words used in the passage also remind us that this perfect reality of wholeness is not just about us, individually. Look at the language: He will live with "them," they will be his "peoples," and he will wipe not just my tears away, but "every tear from *their* eyes." We're going to experience these things together. True shalom is corporate.

In this passage, John is describing what awaits those who by faith use their freedom to follow Christ and not their own way. But John also reminds us that only those who place their faith in Christ get this life of peace, and flourishing. Those who choose a life without God are given what they desired—an eternity without him.

Far too often, we share a truncated gospel. We start with sin and end with the resurrection. But the truth is, the gospel goes from shalom to shalom. The gospel is the good news that the God who created us to dwell with him didn't give up on us. He didn't cast us aside or start over. Instead, he faithfully walked with humanity to bring about his plan of salvation. We who are undeserving of anything from God can live in his perfect environment of wholeness and flourishing forever.

This is the good news—the truer and better story that outshines all the other false stories of this world—that we need to proclaim to help those who have yet to believe. But it's also one we need to rehearse ourselves daily.

Living It Out

Our culture is creative, crafty, and patient with the options it presents us. Rather than giving us everything up front, slowly over time, it shows us pieces of its false stories—each one building on the last, shaping us along the way. In order to resist these false narratives, we must start interacting with each story's content purposefully. We have to start asking questions like: *What is this telling me about God? What is this telling me about myself? How is this story defining hell or heaven—and what is the "Savior" bridging the gap between the two? Where is this telling me the good life can be found?* As we start to see the answers clearly, we can begin to compare them to the truth of the gospel.

But we don't only need to ask good questions. We need to embed our life in the story of the Bible, ordering our lives in such a way as to train our hearts to believe that the best life we could ever have is only found through Jesus. I have already shown you this quote in the introduction, but I'll repeat Josh Chatraw's words here as we conclude our time together:

> Contrasting the Christian story with these rival narratives sobers us to the way we are actually living despite what we confess. To counter these stories, we must embed our lives in the true story. Through the reading of the Scriptures, the fellowship of the saints, the partaking of the sacraments, daily prayers, and the preaching of the Word, God reorients the way we see the world. Constantly comparing the rival stories to God's story is essential to not being lulled to sleep in a secular age.[14]

As I've mentioned previously, the types of habits Chatraw mentions here have been practiced by believers for centuries, and they are called by a certain name: a rule of life. A rule of life is an intentional plan for how a habit will be used to order one's life around the truth of the gospel. This includes habits they will practice on a daily, weekly, monthly, and annual basis. It helps believers decide how they will reclaim the ordinary moments of life to form their hearts and minds to believe that the way of Jesus is better. And as you well know by now,

I intentionally built some of those habits into each chapter of this book on purpose—because I don't just want you to identify when a false story is being whispered in your ear. I want you to have exactly the practices you need to push back against their lies and break free from their hold on you. I want you to exit those false stories and re-enter in the true story—the better story. With each prayer, Bible reading, season of fasting, act of service, moment of confession, and "family gathering" fellowship time with fellow church members, we do just that. We re-enter the story of God, and we proclaim to ourselves, and the world, that the gospel of Jesus Christ is better.

> We proclaim that a peace rooted in God's sovereignty is better than a peace rooted in what we can control.
>
> We proclaim that our given identity as an image-bearer is better than any identity we could earn.
>
> We proclaim that self-sacrificial love is better than selfish love.
>
> We proclaim that merciful justice is better than merciless vengeance.
>
> We proclaim that a joy that comes from God is better than the joy we get from the overconsumption of his creation.

> We proclaim that facing our pain with hope rooted in truth is better than avoiding it with escapism.
>
> We proclaim that a life surrendered to Christ is better than a life of freedom that is surrendered to self.

We order our lives in such a way that we are constantly reminded of why the gospel is better and how it is the only way to experience the good life we all desire.

A Few Final Words . . .

This is a book that has been stirring in me for years. It is the product of a long journey of wrestling with why the Christian faith I claimed was worth holding onto. This wrestling began in my youth, specifically during Sunday school. I remember being at church one Sunday hearing my peers argue with the teacher about why cheating wasn't wrong. Now, I knew enough to know that this was ridiculous, but I was struck at how my teacher didn't immediately shut down the conversation. Instead, they kept it going, indulging the convoluted thinking suggested by the folks in my class. It seemed like a low bar was being set for Christianity. In this moment, it seemed that being a Christian was equated with a watery form of morality. As long as you were good in the world's eyes, you could "make it in."

I was immediately turned off by the conversation. There was something in me that told me there was *more* to my

Christian faith than what was in this room. And for the next fifteen to twenty years, I would spend my time searching for the "more." The thing is, I didn't know exactly what it was and I didn't know where to find it, but I hoped that by digging deep into the Scriptures and being around others who did the same, I would see that my Christian faith was more than just checking a box but was something worth giving my life for.

My pursuits took me to seminary and several different churches that showed me what it meant to live my faith. But it wasn't until I learned about the story of the Bible that I found the "more" that I was looking for. When I learned how the whole Bible, from Genesis to Revelation, is at its core a story that goes from shalom to shalom, the entirety of my faith was transformed.

This theological framework clarified my identity and gave me a way to understand the work that God has called me to. It has helped me learn to process my pain and to forgive others, loving them self sacrificially. But even more than that, it helped me see clearly that Jesus was better. There was no amount of money, prestige, material possessions, or anything else that would ever satisfy my heart like him. The life I would have with Jesus is so much more beautiful, and it's a beauty the world would try to counterfeit, but never successfully copy.

Shalom reframes all of Scripture so that every time I read a passage, I see the beauty of the God who made it possible for me. And when I get to the end of the biblical story, which for us is really another beginning, my heart is full of joy, knowing that the peace, wholeness, and delight I have in part right now I will one day experience in full for eternity.

Part of the reason I wrote this book is because I wish someone had told me this truth all those years ago in that youth group meeting. This book is meant to take the theological, biblical, and formational insights I have picked up over the years and show you how they weave together to form a beautiful mosaic of our life in Christ.

If you don't get anything else from this book, I hope you've learned to slow down and think critically about the ways our culture seeks to form you. I also hope you have found some helpful practices to help you break free from those formative influences. And I hope you've learned to slow down and read Scripture with fresh eyes that recognize God's heart for his people.

But most of all, I hope that you realize that shalom—all that wholeness and delight you're looking for—cannot be found in false gospels, false stories, and false promises that bombard you every day. It can only be found through God by faith in Christ because he is the one who created it. The gospel of Jesus Christ is better because it is the best and only way for us to experience a beautiful life, both now and for eternity.

Continue Learning About Spiritual Habits

If you want to learn more about the spiritual disciplines mentioned in this book, I encourage you to check out the following resources:

Prayer: Experiencing Awe and Intimacy with God by Tim Keller

Fervent: A Woman's Battle Plan to Serious, Specific and Strategic Prayer by Priscilla Shirer

Becoming God's Family: Why the Church Still Matters by Carmen Joy Imes

Why Bother with Church?: And Other Questions About Why You Need It and Why It Needs You by Sam Alberry

Horizontal Jesus: How Our Relationships with Others Affect Our Experience with God by Tony Evans

The Gospel Comes with a House Key: Practicing Radically Ordinary Hospitality in Our Post-Christian World by Rosaria Butter

Living Beyond Offense: Doing the Hard Work of Forgiveness God's Way by Yana Jenay Conner

Friend-ish: Reclaiming Real Friendship in a Culture of Confusion by Kelly Nedham

A Hunger for God: Desiring God through Fasting and Prayer by John Piper

His Word in My Heart: Memorizing Scripture For A Closer Walk with God by Janet Pope

Dwell Differently: Overcome Negative Thinking with the Simple Practice of Memorizing God's Truth by Natalie Abbott and Vera Schmitiz

Sacred Rhythms: Arranging Our Lives for Spiritual Transformation by Ruth Haley Barton

Spiritual Disciplines Handbook: Practices That Transform Us by Adele Calhoun

Practicing the Way: Be with Jesus. Become Like Him. Do as He Did by John Mark Comer

Soul Care in African American Practice by Barbara L. Peakcock

Spiritual Disciplines for the Christian Life by Donald S. Whitney

Notes

Introduction

1. Phillip Ozimek et al., "Materialism in social media–More social media addiction and stress symptoms, less satisfaction with life," *Telematics and Informatics Reports* 13 (March 2024), https://doi.org/10.1016/j.teler.2024.100117.

2. "Our Epidemic of Loneliness and Isolation: The U.S. Surgeon General's Advisory on the Healing Effects of Social Connection and Community," US Department of Health and Human Services, 2023, https://www.hhs.gov/sites/default/files/surgeon-general-social-connection-advisory.pdf.

3. "Generation Anxious: Gen Z More Prone to Fear, Uncertainty Than Older Generations," Barna, October 1, 2024, https://www.barna.com/trends/generation-anxious-gen-z-more-prone-to-fear-uncertainty-than-older-generations/.

4. Tony Reinke, *12 Ways Your Phone Is Changing You* (Crossway, 2017) and *The Life We're Looking For: Reclaiming Relationship in a Technological World* by Andy Crouch (Convergent Books, 2022) are two great reads on this topic.

5. Chris Martin, "5 Social Media Stats Pastors Should Know," Lifeway Research, March 3, 2022, https://research.lifeway.com/2022/03/03/5-social-media-stats-pastors-should-know/.

6. American Bible Society, State of the Bible Report 2021, 2022, 2023, 2024. For the most recent 2024 report, see https://1s712.americanbible.org/state-of-the-bible/stateofthebible/State_of_the_bible-2024.pdf.

7. Dru Johnson and Celina Durgin, "Is It Time to Quit 'Quiet Time'?" *Christianity Today*, April 2023, https://www.christianitytoday.com/2023/03/quit-quiet-time-devotions-bible-literacy-reading-scripture/.

8. Ligonier Ministries, State of Theology Survey, 2022, https://thestateoftheology.com/.

9. James K. A. Smith, *You Are What You Love: The Spiritual Power of Habit* (Brazos Press, 2016), 11.

10. Alister McGrath, *Narrative Apologetics: Sharing the Relevance, Joy, and Wonder of the Christian Faith* (Baker Books, 2019), 9.

11. I live in the Bible Belt where church, Jesus, and Christianity are normative influences in our regional culture. I also live in Mega Church Country—a.k.a., Dallas, Texas—so I realize that large numbers don't always correlate to committed disciples—so much so, that our experience of Christianity includes a struggle with nominalism. But since Jesus is still normative down here, when it comes to understanding the false gospels of our culture, I've had to step outside of my familiar territory to hang out with my brothers and sisters who are in more secularized parts of the country, like California and New York City. The pull away from Christianity seems more prominent in these areas of the country as their regional cultures are leaning more into a post-Christian reality. One of the folks I've learned from is Jon Tyson, a pastor in New York City, and I'm indebted to much of his work, as his explanation of the false gospel of our generation is so clear and compelling, especially this framework which comes from this sermon: "Leverage: Life Without Regret," Jon Tyson Sermon, YouTube, January 11, 2024, https://www.youtube.com/watch?v=ETqw5A88Drk (20:48).

12. Carl Trueman, *The Rise and Triumph of the Modern Self: Cultural Amnesia, Expressive Individualism, and the Road to Sexual Revolution* (Crossway, 2020) provides a historical analysis of this modern phenomenon.

13. I have gained a lot of insight about how to present the gospel in an Age of Radical Individualism from Tim Keller, especially his book *How to Reach the West Again: Six Essential Elements of a Missionary Encounter* (Redeemer City to City, 2020).

14. Joshua D. Chatraw, *Telling a Better Story: How to Talk About God in a Skeptical Age* (Zondervan, 2020), 61.

Chapter 1

1. This is not her real name. Her name and the names of the other folks in the stories I mention in this book have been changed to protect their identity.

2. "Dictionary.com's Word of the Year Is . . ." November 25, 2024, https://www.dictionary.com/e/word-of-the-year-2024/#other-words-on-our-shortlist.

3. *Cambridge Dictionary*, "manifest," https://dictionary.cambridge.org/dictionary/english/manifest.

4. Kimberly Zapata, "How to Manifest Anything You Desire," Oprah Daily, July 22, 2022, https://www.oprahdaily.com/life/a30244004/how-to-manifest-anything/. Other notable sources for a traditional understanding of manifesting are: *The Secret* by Rhonda Byrne, *Manifest: 7 Steps to Living Your Best Life* by Roxie Nafousi, and *Super Attractor: Methods For Manifesting A Life Beyond Your Wildest Dreams* by Gabrielle Bernstein.

5. Paul Tripp, *Suffering: Gospel Hope When Life Doesn't Make Sense* (Crossway, 2018), 156–58.

6. Robert A. Armour, *Gods and Myths of Ancient Egypt* (The American University of Cairo Press, 2016), 164.

7. Bill Gaultiere, "Jesus' Solitude and Silence," Soul Shepherding, https://www.soulshepherding.org/jesus-solitude-and-silence/.

8. I want to be sensitive to those of you who might have a significant struggle with anxiety or maybe even have been diagnosed with an anxiety disorder. Prayer is a wonderful spiritual habit, and sometimes through prayer God will reveal to us that we need additional help in the form of counseling or medicine. Please know both of these are blessings from God and a common grace to all humanity.

Chapter 2

1. Carmen Joy Imes, *Being God's Image: Why Creation Still Matters* (IVP Academic, 2023), 26.

2. Imes, *Being God's Image*, 31, quoting Marc Cortez from *ReSourcing Theological Anthropology.*

3. Lindsey Phillips, "Self-diagnosis in a digital world," *Counseling Today*, March 2022, https://www.counseling.org/publications/counseling-today-magazine/article-archive/article/legacy/self-diagnosis-in-a-digital-world.

4. Christopher J. H. Wright, *Old Testament Ethics for the People of God* (IVP Academic, 2004), 28. Quote taken from Christopher Watkin, *Biblical Critical Theory: How the Bible's Unfolding Story Makes Sense of Modern Life and Culture* (Zondervan, 2022), 278.

5. E. Randolph Richards and Richard James, *Misreading Scripture with Individualist Eyes: Patronage, Honor, and Shame in the Biblical World* (IVP Academic, 2020), 8.

6. The word *Christian* (Χριστιᾶνός) is only used three times in the New Testament and was given to believers by non-Christians. However, the word *adelphoi* (ἀδελφοί) and its derivatives is used hundreds of times in the New Testament. Robert E. Van Voorst,

Building Your New Testament Greek Vocabulary (Eerdmans, 1990), 19.

7. Brian Gamel, "Lord's Supper," ed. John D. Barry et al., *The Lexham Bible Dictionary* (Lexham Press, 2016).

Chapter 3

1. For more on the topic of shame see: *Misreading Scripture through Individualist Eyes: Patronage, Honor, and Shame in the Biblical World* by Randolph Richards and Richard James.

2. Richard J. Foster, *Life with God: Reading the Bible for Spiritual Transformation* (HarperOne, 2010), 7–8.

3. Carolyn Custis James, *The Gospel of Ruth: Loving God Enough to Break the Rules* (Zondervan, 2008), 115.

4. Stanley J. Grenz, *Theology for the Community of God* (Eerdmans, 2000), 179.

5. James, *The Gospel of Ruth: Loving God Enough to Break the Rules*, 115–16.

Chapter 4

1. Robert D. Bergen, *1 and 2 Samuel*, The New American Commentary (B&H Publishing Group, 1996), 475.

2. Aaron L. Garriott, "Who Did David Sin Against?" *Tabletalk,* July 6, 2022, https://tabletalkmagazine.com/posts/who-did-david-sin-against-2020-10/.

3. See footnote in the CSB text for Matthew 18:24.

4. See footnote in the CSB text for Matthew 18:28.

5. Paul David Tripp, *Parenting: 14 Gospel Principles That Can Radically Change Your Family* (Crossway, 2024), 195.

Chapter 5

1. Scot McKnight and Laura Barringer, *A Church Called Tov: Forming a Goodness Culture That Resists Abuses of Power and Promotes Healing* (Tyndale, 2020), 87–88.

2. McKnight, *A Church Called Tov*, 8.

3. Chelsea Peng, "Influencer Marketing: Statistics and Skepticism," *Open Journal of Business Management* 11 (March 2023), https://doi.org/10.4236/ojbm.2023.112040.

4. "Causes and Effects of Climate Change," United Nations, https://www.un.org/en/climatechange/science/causes-effects-climate-change, accessed October 25, 2024.

5. "Household Debt and Credit, 2024: Q4," Federal Reserve Bank of New York, released February 2025, https://www.newyorkfed.org/medialibrary/interactives/householdcredit/data/pdf/HHDC_2024Q4.

6. Jen Wilkin, *Abide: A Study of 1, 2, & 3 John* (Lifeway, 2023), 186.

Chapter 6

1. Rush Witt, *I Want to Escape: Reaching for Hope When Life Is Too Much* (New Growth Press, 2022), 70.

2. *The Oxford Dictionary*'s 2024 word of the year was *brain rot.*

3. Gloria Mark, *Attention Span: A Groundbreaking Way to Restore Balance, Happiness and Productivity* (Hanover Square Press, 2023), 15.

Chapter 7

1. Some of the people who fought for our constitutional freedom were also slaveholders, which makes their legacy complex and, at times, hypocritical. Yet they helped establish a system that others would later fight to extend to everyone. From the Women's Suffrage

Movement to the Civil Rights Movement, Americans throughout history have worked to make our founding ideal of freedom a reality for all.

2. Trevin Wax, "Has the American Dream Turned on Itself?" The Gospel Coalition, September 5, 2019, https://www.thegospelcoalition.org/blogs/trevin-wax/american-dream-turned/.

3. Wax, "Has the American Dream Turned on Itself?"

4. The Hebrew word for *Eden* means "joy or delight." See James A. Swanson, *Dictionary of Biblical Languages with Semantic Domains: Hebrew (Old Testament)* (Logos Research Systems, Inc., 1997).

5. T. Desmond Alexander, *From Eden to the New Jerusalem: An Introduction to Biblical Theology* (Kregel, 2008), 78–79.

6. Christopher Watkin, *Biblical Critical Theory: How the Bible's Unfolding Story Makes Sense of Modern Life and Culture* (Zondervan Academic, 2022), 133.

7. Timothy Keller, *The Reason for God: Belief in an Age of Skepticism* (Penguin Books, 2009), 47.

8. Eli Pariser, *The Filter Bubble: How the New Personalized Web Is Changing What We Read and How We Think* (Penguin Books, 2012), 9.

9. Felicia Su Wong, *Restless Devices: Recovering Personhood, Presence, and Place in the Digital Age* (IVP Academic, 2021), 180.

10. Shay Arnon et al., "Research Study: Association of Cyberbullying Experiences and Perpetration with Suicidality in Early Adolescence," National Library of Medicine, June 2022, https://pubmed.ncbi.nlm.nih.gov/35759263/.

11. Timothy Keller, *How to Reach the West Again: Six Essential Elements of a Missionary Encounter* (Redeemer City to City, 2020), 19.

12. If you want to learn more about how the way we think as people in the West has changed over the centuries, read Andrew Wilson, *Remaking the World: How 1776 Created the Post-Christian West* (Crossway, 2023).

13. Keller, *How to Reach the West Again*, 19.

14. Joshua D. Chatraw, *Telling a Better Story: How to Talk About God in a Skeptical Age* (Zondervan, 2020), 61.

also available from

ELIZABETH WOODSON

ALSO AVAILABLE
from B&H

JEN WILKIN
& J. T. ENGLISH

YOU ARE A THEOLOGIAN

AN INVITATION TO KNOW AND LOVE GOD WELL

J. T. ENGLISH

REMEMBER AND REHEARSE

AN INVITATION TO PARTICIPATE IN GOD'S STORY

KYLE WORLEY

FORMED FOR FELLOWSHIP

BECOMING WHAT YOU BEHOLD

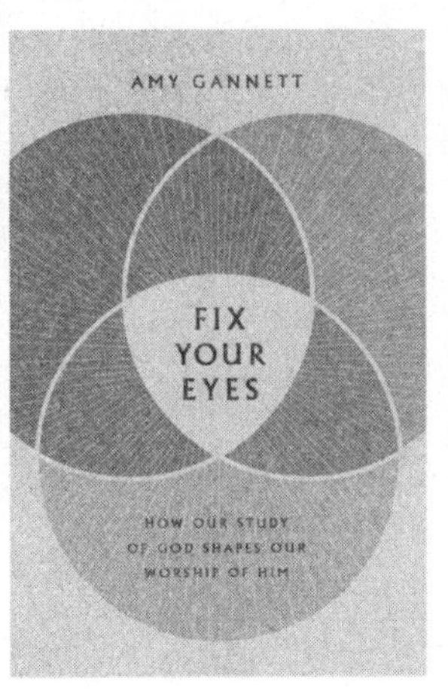